CATHEDRALS & PARKING LOTS

Clemens Starck

Cathedrals & Parking Lots

Collected Poems

Empty Bowl
Anacortes, Washington

Empty Bowl, founded in 1976 as a cooperative letterpress publisher, has produced periodicals, broadsides, literary anthologies, collections of poetry, and books of Chinese translations. As of 2018, our mission is to publish the collected works of poets who share Empty Bowl's founding purpose, "literature & responsibility," and its fundamental theme, the love and preservation of human communities in wild places.

Library of Congress Control Number: 2018952445
ISBN 978-091288-775-3 hardcover
ISBN 978-091288-774-6 paperback

Book design: VJB/Scribe

Empty Bowl
Anacortes, Washington
www.emptybowl.org

This book,
like all my others,
is addressed to
Les Compagnons du Devoir

CONTENTS

JOURNEYMAN'S WAGES

I

Willamette River, Marion St. Bridge: Pier 5, General Details   7
Me and Maloney   8
Putting in Footings   10
Remodeling the House   11
Raising the Grain   12
Journeyman's Wages   14
Job No. 75–14   15
What We Are Doing   16
Slab on Grade   18
In the Meantime   19
The Cathedral   20

II

The Last Evening   23
Man Studying a Map   24
On a Clear Day   25
Tuned In   26
Out of My Head   27
Reading the Gospels in the Lee Hotel   28
The Abandoned Waconda Railroad Station   30
Railroad Crossing   31
Two Chinese Poets
     Mei Yaochen (1002–1058)   32
     Yang Wanli (1127–1206)   33
Regarding the Eclipse   34
Unlacing the Boots   36

III

Admiring the View   39

Through the Haze   40

Moths   41

Looking for Parts   42

A Sunday Drive   44

Butchering Rabbits   45

Snowdrops   46

Cutting the Grass   47

An Invitation   48

Practising Archery   49

IV

Chrysanthemums   53

The Panama Canal   54

Why We Are Afraid   55

Honolulu   56

Ammo Ship   57

Oregon Three Times   58

Commuting   59

Changing the Alternator Belt on Your 504   60

Poem Written in the Parking Lot of a 7-Eleven   62

How It Will Be   63

Falling Off the Roof, I Miss the Falls City Fourth of July
    Parade and Picnic   64

In the Middle of the Night, Waking from a Dream of My
    Children, I Go Downstairs and Read Du Fu   65

Dismantling   66

Prologue	71
Studying Russian on Company Time	74
Making Do	78
Lenin's Typewriter	82
The Museum of Russian History	86
Friendship of the Peoples	90
Дружба Народов	94
Protokol	98
Saving Russia	107
Foxtrot U-521	109

CHINA BASIN

I: *Falsework*

China Basin	115
Gandy Dancing	119
Niagara Cyclo-Massage	120
The Grocery Business	122
Rainer Maria Rilke Goes Construction	126

II: *Camouflage*

The Wisdom of Camouflage	131

III: *Deciding the Course*

Basic Maneuvers	139
Yokohama	140
At Sea	141
Why Buddhists Don't Kill Flies	142

Tulips   143

Airlie Road   144

I Try to Tune In Charles Goodrich...   145

How to Bury a Dead Horse   146

What to Say to Your Neurosurgeon   147

Linguistics   148

Deciding the Course My Education Should Take   149

TRAVELING INCOGNITO

I

Looking for Work: Seven Poems Instead of a Resumé

   1. The Plan   155

   2. Digging Footings   156

   3. Union Pacific   157

   4. Mariposa Slim   158

   5. Eastern Shockcrete   159

   6. *Oil, Paint, and Drug Reporter*   160

   7. The Trade   161

New Orleans, 1958   162

Nevada City, California   163

The *Pan-Oceanic Faith*   164

On the Hook in Manila   166

Leaving Los Angeles   167

II

One of the Locals   171

Driving 99W, Reflecting on War and Solid Waste Disposal 172

Log Trucks and Coyotes   173

Another Poem about Plumbing   174

Why the Old Carpenter Can't Quite Make Out What
    Exactly Is Being Said   175
A Brief Lecture on Door Closers   176
The Chinese Way   178
On My Way to Work I Pass Bud's Auto Wrecking and
    Think about Su Dongpo   179
On the Eve of Retirement I Have This Dream about Going
    Back to Work   180
A Lesson in Physics   181

REMBRANDT, CHAINSAW

Neighbors   185
Building Scaffold   186
The Girl from Panama   187
Gadsky, Elk-Hunting   188
It Could Be Worse   189
Maintenance & Repair   190
Three Sea Stories
    1. On a Freighter, Leaving Newport   191
    2. Saga of the *Goodwill*   192
    3. On the Beach   193
Two Photographs   194
A Few Words about Hope—and Baseball   195
Hitchhiking   196
Otherwise   197
Politician in a Cowboy Hat   198
Echocardiogram   199
Camber   200
Royal Express   201
Immortality   202
Keats and Shelley   204

An Introduction to Russian Grammar   205

A Report from the Provinces   206

Thucydides, Bill O'Reilly and I Discuss Foreign Affairs   207

The Great Books Revisited   208

A Little Meditation on Machines   209

The Authenticity of the Qur'an   210

Late October   211

OLD DOGS, NEW TRICKS

Sanskrit   215

Looking for a Ship   216

A Philosophical Question   218

Taking Leave of Bei Dao on the Sidewalk next to the
     Parking Lot of the Old Church in Downtown Portland   219

Riding the High Ball   220

Snatch Blocks, Curve Balls   222

Life, and Nothing More...   223

Some Random Thoughts on Turning 75   224

Indianapolis   225

Fire and Ice: An Ode to Barbara Stanwyck   226

Patriot   228

The Benefit of Smoking   229

Misha   230

Boundary Dispute   231

Rickreall   232

Long Creek, Walla Walla   234

Derailed by Love   236

El Paso   237

Another Day 241

Splitting the Blanket 242

Like a Pilgrimage 243

How I Became a Red Sox Fan 244

Starting from Lisbon 246

A Short Essay on Trouble 247

Clothes Make the Man 248

Or Maybe Isfahan 249

Notes 251

Acknowledgments 255

Index of Titles 257

Index of First Lines 261

About the Author 265

Poetry presents the thing in order to convey the feeling. It should be precise about the thing and reticent about the feeling, for as soon as the mind responds and connects with the thing the feeling shows in the words; this is how poetry enters deeply into us. If the poet presents directly feelings which overwhelm him, and keeps nothing back to linger as an aftertaste, he stirs us superficially; he cannot start the hands and feet involuntarily waving and tapping in time, far less strengthen morality and refine culture, set heaven and earth in motion and call up the spirits!

—WEI TAI (ELEVENTH CENTURY)

Journeyman's Wages

It is true
that one kind of work is different from another;
but whoever carries out his duty impartially,
for him all work is equal.

— MEISTER ECKHART

I

WILLAMETTE RIVER,
MARION ST. BRIDGE:
PIER 5, GENERAL DETAILS

The sun slams into us
like one of the pile drivers
down on the gravel bar. The crew I'm on
is erecting forms for concrete piers.

Machinery roars. Earth shudders.
Cottonwood leaves turn gray with dust.

Companions of duty,
is this our assignment? Simply to be here, packed
in these heavy bodies, dumbfounded,
while time drags
and the river slides quietly by?

I signal the sun to slack off a little,
but nothing happens.
I keep on signaling anyway.

ME AND MALONEY

Job's nearly over,
me and Maloney all that's left of the crew.
Sunk in the hillside,
hundreds of tons of reinforced concrete
formed in the shape of a drum
ninety-two feet in diameter, eighteen feet deep—
it could be a kiva, or a hat box, or look from the air
like a missile silo.

It could be a storage tank for toxic waste.
It could be a vault to house
the national treasure.

In any case, it's finished,
ready for backfill. Now it's the earth's.

And I'm left with Maloney,
who likes to drink beer after work
and tell stories.
Construction stories. Ex-wife stories. Stories
like how he clubs possums to death with a two-by-four
when he finds them
prowling in back of his warehouse at night.

He laughs, telling the stories.

Maloney quit drinking once.
After a year and nine months he decided he'd rather
die of alcohol
than boredom.

I know what he means. I work
for Maloney Construction.
When it rains we work in the rain. When it snows
we work in the snow.
I am Maloney's right-hand man:
when he laughs, I laugh too.

PUTTING IN FOOTINGS

Jake is the superintendent on this job,
I draw foreman's wages.
Mack the carpenter, Tom the laborer,
and there are others
wet to the skin
and cold to the bone—
that's Oregon in December.

Be joyful, my spirit. Be of high purpose.
We are putting in footings—
slogging through mud, kneeling
in it, supplicants pleading for mercy,
brutal, cursing,
drizzle coming down harder.

This is the Project Site.
Tobacco-chewing men in big machines dig holes,
we build the forms.
Ironworkers tie off rebar.
This concrete we pour could outlast
the Pyramids.

. . . . .

After the weather
has cleared, and the concrete has cured
and the paychecks are spent—

millennia later,
after the Pyramids
have pulverized and Jake has disappeared
and reappeared many times,
as grouchy as ever,
angels will come to measure our work,
slowly shaking their heads.

REMODELING THE HOUSE

The next step was
to tear out the dormer
some half-assed handyman cobbled together,
ruining the lines of this old house,
and build it back again
proper.

Now every true apprentice knows
there are principles to reckon with, spirit
level and plumb bob; so,
I honor the man who taught me
the soul is a house
and you build it,
                    joining the wood,
driving the nails home.

RAISING THE GRAIN

*The grain of rough lumber will show plainly
in the finished concrete even though raising
of grain is prevented by oiling the forms. If
more pronounced grain marks are desired,
the grain can be raised by wetting the lumber
before oiling. A still more effective method is
to spray the sheathing lumber with ammonia.*

— *FORMS FOR ARCHITECTURAL
CONCRETE*, PORTLAND
CEMENT ASSOCIATION, 1952

I

The lot is vacant
except for me
and my toolbox. My toolbox
is huge
and is painted brown. It contains

little racks and holsters,
numerous compartments,
which hold all the tools I'll need for this job,
including a hacksaw.

What am I waiting for?

Everything is ready.

My chisels were dull, but for two hours
I've been sharpening them.

I am holding a hammer.
I am going to drive a nail.

But my hands, my hands are smashed
and bleeding!
The knuckles are raw.

It won't be easy—
it's never as easy as it looks...

—"What are you building, a piano?"

And when I have driven the nail
I am going to clinch it.

Already this year I've built
a Serbian Orthodox
Church,
and a mortuary
(Chapel of the Sunset, 26th Avenue
and Irving). Plus a number of other less tangible
structures.

My union dues are all paid up,
and I plan to continue
in the trade:
bookshelves for a crippled lady, a cage
for a boa constrictor...

The country is
going to hell, but a good mechanic
can always find work.

JOURNEYMAN'S WAGES

To the waters of the Willamette I come
in nearly perfect weather,
Monday morning
traffic backed up at the bridge
a bad sign.
           Be on the job at eight,
boots crunching in gravel;
cinch up the tool belt, string out the cords
to where we left off on Friday—
that stack of old
form lumber, that bucket of rusty bolts
and those two beat-up sawhorses
wait patiently for us.

Gil is still drunk, red-eyed, pretending he's not
and threatening to quit;
Gordon is studying the prints.
Slab on grade, tilt-up panels, Glu-lams
and trusses...

Boys, I've got an idea—
instead of a supermarket
why couldn't this be a cathedral?

JOB NO. 75–14

for Ron Boyce

Drive stakes, shoot grades,
get a big Cat to scalp and scrape and gouge:
contour the site for proper drainage.
Berm and swale.

Rough-grade it then, with
a blade, and hope
it don't rain. Set hubs,
haul in base rock, grade it again, then
pave it with a thick crust of blacktop
to make a parking lot.
                            I'm building
a new Safeway, in West Salem,
for some religious millionaire,
and we will all buy our groceries there.

"Well, tomorrow's Friday," I say
to the guy who looks like Jesus driving stakes
and rod-hopping for me,
and he says, "Yeah, then two!
and then five and then two and then five…"

Seven being a magic number
and the earth having a thin skin,
we make motions to bow
ceremoniously, but instead, a couple of
unmasked accomplices, confederates
on a losing planet,
we look at each other
and grin—
            which means: "to draw back the lips
so as to show the teeth
as a dog in snarling,
or a person in laughter or pain."

WHAT WE ARE DOING

What we are doing is hard to explain.
It would take diagrams and curse words, complicated
facial expressions
and lengthy descriptions of little-known tools. It would be
like trying to explain *quarks* and *leptons*
to someone who had merely asked
where the restrooms were.

However, to put it simply,
Davey and I
are on the fifth floor of the library, working
partners, jockeying stepladders
back and forth in the narrow aisles between the stacks,
not soaking up knowledge, but Pop-
riveting ceiling grid.

Davey has his ladder, I have mine; each
of us has a small vise-grips.
From Microbiology to Astrophysics,
dragging our tools and our bodies along with us,
we push on
inexorably, zigzagging
through the Dewey decimal system.

Pausing for a moment in Immunology,
naturally I think of Holub
peering into his microscope, making a poem
out of lymphocytes!
By the time we reach *The Bella Coola River Estuary*
and *Holocene Carbonate Sedimentation*,
it's noon, and time for lunch.

And cards! The game
has been going on for years,
at least since the time of the Pyramids, if not coeval
with carbonate sedimentation.
Five-card draw, jokers wild. We ante up...
Frank's three queens beat my two pair.
Davey's deal.

The afternoon will be a scorcher.

SLAB ON GRADE

At dawn the concrete trucks
are already there: revving their engines,
rumbling and throbbing, one by one
maneuvering into position.
Enormous insects,
on command
they ooze from their huge revolving abdomens
a thick gray slime.

Insects attending to insects,
the crew fusses over them, nursing wet concrete
into the forms.

Someone to handle the chute,
a couple laborers mucking, one pulling mesh, and two
finishers working the screed rod—
this is called pouring
slab on grade.

What could be flatter or more nondescript
than a concrete slab?
For years people will walk on it,
hardly considering that it was put there
on purpose,
on a Thursday in August
by men on their knees.

IN THE MEANTIME

Spiritual efforts may come to nothing;
right behavior's not easy to form.
In the workshop I put my tools in order
and sweep the floor—
sawdust and shavings, three bags full.

Idly I pick up a handsaw,
inspecting the blade for true.
This saw has a life, it uses my hands
for its own purpose. Lucky,
to know your own uses!

In the meantime I stay busy.
Emery cloth and steel wool
will take the rust off metal. Linseed oil
rubbed into the handles
keeps the wood alive.

THE CATHEDRAL

The decree was issued. A cathedral was to be built. *Ad majorem gloriam Dei*, etc. Workmen were chosen on the basis of their skill and their devotion to the Holy Faith. The foundations were laid, the walls begun. A scaffolding was erected, and tier by tier the great stones were set in place. As the walls rose, the scaffold rose alongside them.

Years passed. The structure was completed. Gargoyles, stained glass, flying buttresses—altogether an imposing achievement.

For centuries the stone nave absorbed the confessions of widows and murderers, followed by their urgent prayers for divine intercession. A plaster statue of the Virgin was said to have blushed once, and thus sanctity was embellished by a hint of the miraculous. The stoup for holy water, worn thin by daily usage, had to be replaced three times.

"Spiritual decay" (or an equally vague phrase) is the usual explanation for the rapid decline of the cathedral-building civilization. An exact chronology has never been fixed, but the already dilapidated cathedral was finally reduced to a pile of rubble. From time to time children playing among the stones discovered what later were determined to be religious artifacts. These were claimed by the authorities and removed to museums.

The site of the cathedral would long ago have been put to more productive uses were it not for a singular phenomenon: towering above the ruins and completely encircling them, there remained the wooden scaffolding used by the original builders. This had never been torn down. It remains to this day, testimony to the marvelous wit and ingenuity of those ancient people.

II

THE LAST EVENING

Rainer Maria Rilke, "Letzter Abend"

Night and the furthest distance; and the sword,
the army passing, at whose command they were...
He only glanced then from the harpsichord,
continuing to play, and looked at her

as in a mirror at himself: afraid
and unafraid, so flushed with youth, and knowing
no youthful promise could prevent his going,
sweet and seductive as the notes he played.

Then suddenly—as if the glass had broken!
She rose, about to speak, the words unspoken,
and heard the pounding of her heart instead.

His music died. Outside a breeze protested.
And motionless on the polished table rested
the stiff black shako with the white death's head.

MAN STUDYING A MAP

There's a picture I have.
I've had it for years. My mother
had it before me.
An elderly English gentleman
in riding boots and scarlet jacket
sitting, knees apart,
on the edge of an old-fashioned horsehair couch.
Spread out on the floor in front of him
is a map at which he is pointing
with the tip of his long-stemmed pipe.

The room is dark
except for the glow from the fireplace
and light from a narrow window
high in the wall behind the couch.

I took him for my grandfather,
and always thought he must have been imprisoned there
in that dim room.
But now when I visit him he explains
there's no reason for me to be sad
for his sake. He has
all he needs: tobacco, couch, a crackling fire
and the map.

ON A CLEAR DAY

From Telegraph Hill you can see for miles
on a clear day. Today
is May 7, 1965. Overhead, flying in tight formation,
three jet fighters are practising
for war.

The morning papers have already faded.
Their headlines
threaten me from ten yards away. Is it true
the Marines have landed?

For some reason
I keep picturing to myself
the sod huts
of homesteaders in the Dakotas,
and buffalo herds,
while the ghost of Coolidge addresses a convocation
of the Daughters of the American Revolution,
the D.A.R.

Imagine!
The American Revolution!
Bunker Hill, the long winter of '77, Washington
crossing the Delaware...

Anyway, it's all over.
Now we are crossing the Red Sea—we,
the Egyptians.

TUNED IN

The News is between 94 and 92
on my radio dial. I listen to it every
evening. I like
to keep informed.
In the morning I listen to it again,
the same News, re-broadcast.
I have a tape recorder, and I record the News,
play it back
at odd hours of the day,
and at night when I can't sleep.
People call, ask me
what I've been doing. I say
"I've been listening to the News."
Of course it's not always so easy. My dial
needs constant adjustment.
For whole days I get nothing but static,
and I think
it's the universe crackling.
But when I'm tuned-in, I'm happy.
I listen
impassively—I know how important it is
to remain calm.
                    Even so, even so,
I nearly have an orgasm
every time a junta is overthrown.
I hate juntas.

Who do they think they're kidding?

Not me! I never
go out of the house—I don't have to.
There are maps tacked to my walls,
and I know
what's happening, everywhere.

OUT OF MY HEAD

I have a head, a noble
little skull.
Of all my possessions I love it the most.
More than my books or my bolo knife,
more than my tools,
more, even, than my entire collection
of petrified wood.

It's not in A-1 condition—the teeth
are rotten, the skin's a little tight
across the forehead—
but it's mine,
and I'm not complaining.

My head is my friend:
it talks to me,
it tells me what I want to hear.

Sometimes we go on trips together,
and it's fun.

It used to be different.
I lived in it then, like an animal
huddled in a cave.
But sooner or later you have to come out.
I don't know why.
Because you do, because you do...

So I did, and now I'm out.

I can do anything now, I'm free
to go anywhere. But whatever I do,
wherever I go,
I carry my head in my hands.

READING THE GOSPELS
IN THE LEE HOTEL

I

"Panorama Land" the tourist folders
call this place: the country hereabouts
unfolds, range after snowy range
in all directions,
and after that, clouds.

According to the account of what happened
as narrated by John,
in this translation,
Jesus said,
        "I came into this world
so that people might be set asunder,
so that those who cannot see should see,
and those who can see
should become blind."

2

I came here looking for a place to settle,
hopeful this might be it
this time,
        traveling from a distant constellation
to be here in this room, a newcomer
strange to the local customs.

And so it was. I was reading *The Four Gospels*,
listening to music through the static
on a San Francisco station...

3

Wallpaper peeling, woodwork encrusted with paint,
one bare lightbulb dangling
by its wires from the high ceiling...
End of the line
for lonesome travelers, down and out.
One flight up, over the bar.
Lee Hotel.
      A drunk lurches, singing,
down the hall—body
trying clumsily to follow
the moves its spirit makes.
The radiator hisses.

"For judgment
I am come into this world" is how
the King James Version renders the passage.

4

After midnight I go out,
bundled in checkered mackinaw and wool watch cap,
to walk the icy main street—
four blocks up, and five blocks back
on the other side, to an all-night café.

"Cheeseburger and coffee," I say
to the faded waitress.
            She's new in town herself,
she says, moving with accomplished grace
behind the counter
toward the stainless steel coffee urn.

THE ABANDONED
WACONDA RAILROAD STATION

No roof left at all, stone walls
dilapidated, blackberries creeping through
the empty windows—
it looks like one of those engravings
in an old book, of a ruined Roman villa,
or rather, an eighteenth-century
English landscape architect's idea
of a ruined Roman villa;

that is, if in your mind
you can mask out
the thick stand of second- or third-growth
Douglas fir, and the ghosts of wistful travelers
still standing in line
to buy a one-way ticket to Portland.

RAILROAD CROSSING

Just turned 20,
riding the freights through Oregon...
Came this way once, on these same tracks, lounging
in the doorway of an empty boxcar
rolling a cigarette,
waving nonchalantly at people in cars.

Twenty years later,
at the grade crossing on State Street, in Salem,
I squint impatiently into the afternoon sun,
engine idling,
waiting for a train to pass.

TWO CHINESE POETS

Mei Yaochen (1002–1058)

Mei Yaochen extolled the "even and bland."
His famous poem on the river-pig fish he wrote impromptu
after having dinner at Fan Zhongyan's.
Difficult scenes he could describe nonchalantly,
showing no signs of technical skill.
To aspiring poets who submitted their work
he would send a poem in reply.
For example,
in the one called "Reading
the Poetry Scroll of Magistrate Zhang," he says:
Although I have not allowed myself to become inattentive while reading them,
I cannot understand one out of ten!

Yang Wanli (1127–1206)

Yang Wanli was much praised
for his "live method" of composition.
His friend Ge Tianmin wrote:
Yang understands how to make a dead snake leap with life.

Esteemed as one of the Four Masters etc.,
enlightened at 51,
he became even more matter-of-fact.
Regarding the immortal Li Bai's celebrated observation
    that Jade Mountain
falls over by itself without anyone pushing,
he said flatly: *Who gives a damn*
whether Jade Mountain falls over or not?

REGARDING THE ECLIPSE

Chances are I'll never tell
the story of how I found myself
adrift at sea
in a twelve-foot dinghy with a single oar;
or how, once, in the mountains
called Sierra Nevada,
trapped on a snowbound freight train,
my intrepid companions and I
existed for several days
on a fifty-pound sack of frozen marshmallows.

In retrospect
you could call it adventure, but at the time
it was nothing special. Anyway,
some events—like cloud formations
or teenage children—
are completely inexplicable.

My ambitions were nebulous at best.
All I ever wanted to be was a glassblower
or a wood carver
or failing that, a utility infielder.
A career in the Foreign Service
looked promising once, but I couldn't feature myself
in formal attire
on a balcony overlooking the capital...
What would I be doing there?
Serving cocktails
to the Peruvian attaché's voluptuous wife?

And so it is that I stand
on the sagging porch of a tumbledown house
regarding the lunar eclipse
through binoculars held steady by my stalwart left hand.
With the other I gesticulate wildly,
but fail to observe
any change
in the shadow cast by this earth on the moon.

UNLACING THE BOOTS

Unlacing my boots, I ease my feet into moccasins.
Soap and warm water absolve the skin from grime.
On the desk in my study are stacks of books—
ancient poems and other accounts
of men who lived on this planet once.
A good chunk of oak on the fire
will take the chill off my bones.

III

ADMIRING THE VIEW

Hummingbirds live in the thicket.
So do blackberries, roses, and flowering quince.
Just after sunrise the birds dart out,
buzzing and flashing
like tiny machines.

Like soap flakes
white rose petals melt on the lawn.
Minutes pass... Then hours, days, years.
When visitors come they admire the view.
I don't disagree.

Green hills. Blue sky. No clouds.

On the ridge to the east a hillside
has been logged off. Out over the valley
vultures circle,
soaring, riding the updrafts,
adjusting their great wings.

THROUGH THE HAZE

Old stories, poems, the dictionary—
sure, I read books,
but forget what I read, so what good does it do?
Studying, musing, staying up half the night...
Some say it's worthwhile, but it may
just be odd.

Alone for the day in an empty house.
Hot afternoon. I fall asleep...
and wake up with a headache, flies still buzzing,
the evening sky suffused with an eery yellow light.
The haze is so thick the hills are dim.
Things I was going to do I didn't do.
Four hours blank.

Fumbling for consciousness,
half-disbelieving the clock—how remote
it all seems now,
the lure of literature, and the singular hope
that words will clarify my life.

MOTHS

In the pump house where I go
to escape the TV
and the savagery of family life,
I share a lightbulb with the moths.
They flutter. I read.

Or vice versa: they
are studying the light. That fierce white incandescence
interests them.
My blue eyes flutter across the page
like two pale moths.

When it's working right the pump cuts in
at 20 p.s.i.
          Meanwhile I try
to pronounce correctly
the names, in Chinese, of the Five Classics.

The moths are excited. Moth dust
settles impalpably
in the forest of hair on the back of my hand.

At 40 the pump cuts out. Now
I can hear myself talking—but still
can't quite tell
what it is that is being said.

LOOKING FOR PARTS

I

Leaning on the counter of the local
auto parts store,
a man is telling a story
about a clutch.

What *I'm* after is a left front
shock absorber bracket
for my pickup. He's only looking
for conversation.

He looks like Humphrey Bogart
with a blotchy face. I probably
look odd myself.

"Those old Chevys were good trucks,"
we agree. Our lives
are linked by machines.

2

They don't have the part,
but I get one from the wrecker:
left hand gloved in leather
to hold the cold chisel, right hand brandishing
a maul...
                Down on one knee in the weeds,
bent over a wrecked truck chassis,
I notice the ground is soaked
with crankcase oil
and littered with nuts and bolts.

Straightening up, I can see
a black dog chained

to an old yellow school bus. Acres of scrapmetal
flaking with rust.
A goldfinch flits through a thistle patch.

3

A plywood and tar-paper shack
has *OFFiCE* lettered crudely over the door.
Inside, a counter
unbelievably cluttered, a miniature junkyard
behind which the burly proprietor sits,
an immortal in greasy coveralls
chewing on a cigar. He says
he sold his yard in Junction City
to buy this one.
                        Over his pocket, stitched in red,
is the one word: *Jim.*

4

Directly behind the stitching
in the chamber formed by a cage of bone
is the man's heart.
I hand him three dollars
and climb in my truck.
                        It's not fog
that reduces visibility now,
but streams of white fluff blown by the wind—
a snowstorm in August, each flake
a whole galaxy.
Thistledown! thistledown!

Mulling this over, I cruise down the highway.
Hands rest lightly on the wheel.
Oil changed, new plugs and points—pickup
running like a charm.

A SUNDAY DRIVE

The highway out of Salem
crosses the Willamette and skirts the Eola Hills.
It goes to the coast,
a foot-thick, forty-foot-wide asphalt strap
edged with gravel, weeds
and the bodies of small animals.
In places the earth has been gouged
to receive it.

On Sundays people go for a drive.
Following the signs for Ocean Beaches, an hour or so,
in no time they're there.
Park. Get out and stretch
and walk for a while,
leaving shoe-prints in the wet sand.
Later the kids want to stop for pizza.

If it's autumn, the drive home will be spectacular.
Fog settles in the hollows.
Woodsmoke merges with the fog.
Mountains of shaggy green-black fir forest
set off the hardwoods—
maples' fiery yellow,
oak leaves touched with rust.

BUTCHERING RABBITS

To kill one with a single blow takes force.
It leaves them limp, stretched out in the grass
without a tremor,
white and black and reddish brown,
a trickle of blood from the nostrils—
nameless *things, that* used to be called
Ginger, Popcorn, Snowball, Liz...

Skin clings tenaciously to the carcass;
flesh is soft but hard to carve.
My knives are sharp, but unlike Cook Ding
my skill is slight.

Fortunately my wife will transform all this
death to some purpose.
Her rabbit stew is incomparable.

SNOWDROPS

In February my children pick snowdrops
and put them to float in a dish of water. Small
white petals streaked with green,
you are like my children, floating,
floating on clear water.

CUTTING THE GRASS

When the power mower quits
I pick up the scythe
and attack the vegetation like a storm-trooper,
cutting a swath in the overgrown yard.
My children rake and fork it into piles,
not without grumbling a little,
but mildly.

All afternoon, with breaks for lemonade,
we give the place a haircut.
Grass piles multiply.
Hollows and hummocks appear.
Avoiding his shadow
the black cat steps gingerly through the stubble.
A single yellowjacket mirrors
what's left of the sun.

My father had a scythe
identical to this one: standing there, wiping his brow
with a white handkerchief.

Come closer, children,
this is the Kingdom of Heaven.
Look!
      (I should mention also,
sweet as it was,
for dessert that night we had chocolate pudding.)

AN INVITATION

Friends, if you'll stop by sometime
I'll take off this serious face.
We'll smoke
and get into some blackberry wine—
this year's batch
is just right!
        My old neighbor the moon
will climb out of the hills,
happy to join us.
Yardlights a mile away in the valley
will be no closer
than the nearest star.

Half-lit ourselves, we'll sit
on the veranda
telling preposterous stories.
Like the one that begins:
        "Long ago
on this planet there was a man,
an ordinary man…"

A country place is quiet at night.
In the woods sometimes an owl,
or coyotes—upstairs,
one of the kids must be having a dream.

PRACTISING ARCHERY

Mist in the firs. Moss on the oaks.
The weather, this time of year, is impossible.
Snow on the mountains—no,
those are clouds!

Two little Chinamen, kneeling,
one is in brick-colored pajamas, the other
in charcoal-colored pajamas, each
drawing a bow...
     What's this all about,
the young Buddha practising archery?

Everywhere dark firs
stick straight up
through lighter moss-green oaks. White
patches of mist float down the hillsides
from higher elevations.
Oregon is not so far from China.

The archers kneel, their bows pulled taut.
Their aim is true. There are no arrows
fitted to the string.
There is little, really, to worry about,
but I still do.

IV

CHRYSANTHEMUMS

Yellow and orange, so heavy with rain
they have to be tied in bunches and fastened
by baling twine
to the side of the shed. And mistletoe,
dark knots of it visible now
high in the bare oaks. Underfoot,
a mattress of soggy leaves.

On my birthday I get up early,
stirred by a vague excitement.
"It's snowing, it's snowing!" the children exclaim.
First snow of the year.

Approaching fifty a man starts
counting backwards.
After driving the kids to school in town
I stop for gas. While Stu fixes
the loose windshield wiper
we touch on lung cancer, carburetor trouble,
this thing and that.

THE PANAMA CANAL

My neighbor, an out-of-work welder,
is of the opinion that—well, you take for example
the Panama Canal...
"It was ours!" he keeps saying.
"It was built with our own sweat and blood!"

He would never have given it away
as our spineless President did.

All week it's been raining.
Jobs are scarce and he's been laid off.
However, he believes
the new President, a hard-liner,
will get this country back where it should be.

"Of course," he concedes
with a boyish grin, "there might be war."
But he doesn't think the Russians
will put up much of a fight.

While we talk, I can hear his wife
inside, vacuuming.

WHY WE ARE AFRAID

My family is bored. We have everything.
There's nothing left for us to have, except maybe
a space shuttle
or an automatic ice-cube maker.
Verily, merchandise breeds merchandise.
Every day new catalogues arrive.
But it's no use. Whatever they're selling
we've already got.

My country, too, is bored. Even more so, because
it has the space shuttle
and it can make ice cubes at a prodigious rate.
And that is why we're so afraid,
and why we need
bombers that can fly through the eye of a needle,
bullets that travel backwards and forwards,
crossbows
and harquebuses
to protect us from our enemies.

What I say is: Enemies, when you arrive
you can have it all! I'll leave
instructions for the microwave
next to the sink in the bottom drawer.

HONOLULU

It was all new to me!
When the crew messman went berserk
we were three days at sea,
Long Beach
to Yokosuka on an MSTS charter.

First we had to catch him—he was fast
and crazy. Then
he was straitjacketed, sedated, and chained
to a bunk in the ship's infirmary.

Under new orders
we changed course, steamed north
for Honolulu; docked
two days later,
put him off, and took on bunkers there.

That night, standing gangway watch,
the warm Hawaiian air
redolent with the smell of diesel fuel,
I thought of the crew messman.

Both his arms were covered with tattoos—
dragons and roses,
names of women,
elaborate patterns of blue
and red.

AMMO SHIP

Mostly we hauled asphalt,
tens of thousands of drums of asphalt.
The master plan
called for Southeast Asia to be a parking lot.
If it wasn't asphalt, it was bombs.
The bombs were for the enemy.

One trip, four days out of Southern California
in heavy seas, the cargo began to shift.
We climbed down into the hold with shoring timbers
         and wedges.
The bombs in their fragile wooden crates
tossed about like restless sleepers,
a nightmare screech of nails pulling and wood
splintering.
               The rest of the trip
morale was low. Not even
the cook's special blueberry pancakes
helped.

The people the bombs were for
scattered. Deer at the start of hunting season,
they knew we were coming
and they were scared, too.

OREGON THREE TIMES

1

The first time was on a freight train
from Utah. (I was headed for Kansas City,
but got turned around.)
At Klamath Falls a railroad dick
probed the boxcar with a flashlight:
"Any coons in there?"

2

The second time I had a wife
and an old Buick.
We drove up from California.
For recreation I bought a fishing rod and reel
at a sporting goods store in Springfield.
I've still got the reel.

3

The third time: a merchant ship
just in from the Far East.
Longshoremen loaded us with lumber at Newport
in the rain.
We all went into town. Got drunk.
It was our own country.

COMMUTING

Firs on the hillside:
mist drifts through them like smoke.
White mist, black trees...
Headlights sweep the wet pavement.
Waiting at home
my son—he's ten, he wants to know
what we're here for.
Black firs. White mist.
Loose tools rattle in the back of the truck.
In twenty miles I ought to be able
to figure out something.

CHANGING THE ALTERNATOR BELT
ON YOUR 504

I

To do this the radiator
must be removed. Two bolts on top, three
on the bottom, then disconnect
the hoses.
Four small screws, and the shroud
comes loose. This leaves
the radiator free.

Lift it out carefully. Set it
outside the garage, on the gravel.
Take five.
Smoke.
Contemplate the plum tree.

2

If the soul took shape
it might look like that—a cloud of white blossoms
throbbing with bees...
In the rank grass,
daffodils flaunt their yellow message.
Six fat robins
skitter across the pasture.

It makes no sense.
Eddie Rodriguez is dying. You know
that you are dying too,
and still there is spring
and fixing cars.

3

With the radiator out,
the rest is easy.
After replacing the belt, reverse the procedure:
radiator, hoses, antifreeze.

Turn on the ignition.
Be brave. Be sad. Check for leaks.
Wipe your greasy hands on a rag.
Drive on,
brother, drive on.

for E.R., 1945–1987

POEM WRITTEN IN THE PARKING LOT
OF A 7-ELEVEN

No breeze to ruffle the maple leaves.
The hills at the edge of town
are brown. Toy cars
slide up to the 7-Eleven,
and stop. A delivery van is delivering
video games.

Also to be observed
are the conformation of clouds, the proximity
of mountains,
and the absence of gunfire.

On their way home from school
children loiter,
sucking refreshment from large paper cups
that say *Pepsi*—
white, red, and blue.

. . . . .

The afternoon
develops slowly. Every so often,
agitated by passing traffic,
a scrap of paper
drifts to the west, and then to the east.

Like answers to irrelevant questions,
a few blocks away, gathering speed,
trucks hurtle by
on their way out of town.

HOW IT WILL BE

Heavy rains. The river swollen.
Soldiers in rubber rafts. On the bank, a horse's
bloated carcass,
and the sprawled remains
of those who manned a machine-gun nest.

Wartime photograph.
Caption reads: "Partisans crossing the Drina,
May 1943."

One of the soldiers looks like my uncle.
Rifle slung over his shoulder, he is reciting
the Ten Commandments,
or else he is telling the others
how it will be
after the war.

Are they advancing or retreating?
Is there hope, or is this desperation?
Nothing is clear.
Gray skies. The water muddy.

One of my uncles *was* a soldier—
Fort Benning, Georgia... Germany... then Japan.
Another preached the word of God.
The third was a janitor.

FALLING OFF THE ROOF, I MISS
THE FALLS CITY FOURTH OF JULY
PARADE AND PICNIC

X-rays negative, I limp across the parking lot.
Driving home I remember my father telling
how my grandfather used to make a patriotic speech
to his congregation
every year on the Fourth.
Later I learn that my elder daughter
came in second in the sack race.

IN THE MIDDLE OF THE NIGHT, WAKING FROM A DREAM OF MY CHILDREN, I GO DOWNSTAIRS AND READ DU FU

Troubles erupt—like a skin rash.
Worry gnaws at the innards, a belligerent
ulcer.
     In twelve hundred years
no parent has ever
found a solution for this.

I stoke the fire. Smoke
sucked up the chimney
resembles a prayer or a curse.
Spurned by forty publishers, my poems
go unread.

So is it any wonder
the doctor says, "You'll be taking these pills
for the rest of your life."

DISMANTLING

Call Joel (eves) 623-9765

Smack in the public eye
at Ninth and Van Buren, tearing down
an old house—
"Not demolition, dismantling!" says Joel. Slowly
we make the house disappear.
It takes a few months.
We do this for a living.
                       Our sign says:
USED LUMBER FOR SALE.
Neat stacks of it on the front lawn
around a dormant forsythia—
shiplap and siding, and over here
we have two-by...
That pile is already sold.

We also have toilets, sinks, remarkable
savings on bent nails,
French doors, free kindling
and more. Lots more.

        · · · · ·

With the roof off
a house looks more like a cathedral,
rafters outlined against the sky.
A pair of ragged priests,
stick by stick we celebrate
nothing. We are making the shape of nothing,
creating
an absence.

And when we have finished,
what will there be at Ninth and Van Buren?
A square of bare earth
where a house was.
Sidewalk. Foundation. Concrete stoop.
Two steps up
and you're there.

Studying Russian on Company Time

Умом Россию не понять,
Аршином общим не измерить;
У ней особенная стать—
В Россию можно только верить.

— Ф.И. ТЮТЧЕВ

You can't grasp Russia with your mind,
By ordinary means she can't be measured;
Her character is one-of-a-kind—
To fathom Russia you must believe.

—F.I. TYUTCHEV, 1866

PROLOGUE

The day before I began studying Russian I had no intention whatsoever of studying Russian. It was the last thing on my mind. I had no particular interest in Russia or things Russian. Except for Chekhov, of course, and Dostoevsky. And learning the Cyrillic alphabet always seemed like it might be a good thing to do... But I was certainly not a Russophile.

It was September 1991. Astonishing events were taking place in Eastern Europe. The coup attempt against Gorbachev had triggered what would have been unthinkable a few weeks earlier: the collapse of the Soviet Union. I was teaching an evening class at a local university and, as it turned out, I was to share an office with a visiting professor just off the plane from Moscow. Here was my chance to get a firsthand account of what was happening over there. Unfortunately, my office partner could speak very little English. Conversation was severely limited. So, in frustration, I offered to help her with her English, and as a joke I suggested that she could teach me Russian in return.

What began as a joke soon turned into an obsession, a daily practice. Phonetics. Grammar. Vocabulary. Something about the Russian language itself intrigued me. Trying to mouth the sounds of it was addictive. Only later, through the language, did I become fascinated with Russian culture and Russian history. And eventually I went to Russia.

The following pages are a little travelogue of sorts—some poems composed along the path of that continuing obsession, together with the context out of which they arose.

~

As well as an obsession, studying Russian was for me a kind of subterfuge, a clandestine adventure. It was an unlikely thing to be doing, sitting in my truck at work on my day job, during coffee breaks and at lunch time, flipping through Russian flash cards or conjugating Russian verbs aloud. It was a way of sneaking something completely arbitrary and improbable into my life. It felt almost illicit.

This first poem is conspiratorial in tone. It marks the 75th anniversary of the Bolshevik Revolution, an event that few were celebrating at the time.

By way of notes:

THE PERIOD OF STALIN'S PURGES in the late '30s is known as the Great Terror. One of its victims was the Civil War hero and marshal of the Red Army, M. N. Tukhachevsky. The question may arise: Had the officer corps of the Red Army not been decimated by the purges, would the German tanks ever have gotten as far as Stalingrad in 1940?

IN APRIL 1917, shortly after the February Revolution had overthrown the tsar, V. I. Lenin returned from exile in Switzerland, arriving in St. Petersburg to a tumultuous welcome. The Finland Station is the *gare du nord* in St. Petersburg, the terminal for trains to and from the north.

THE FOUR RUSSIAN WORDS in the poem are simply the first four days of the week: Monday, Tuesday, Wednesday, Thursday.

STUDYING RUSSIAN ON COMPANY TIME

Act like you're reading the sports page.
Pretend your textbook's a sandwich, and start eating it.
When the foreman asks what you're doing, ask him
if he knows where Olga and Ivan are.
Enunciate carefully: Olga
and Ivan are not in the library, Olga and Ivan
were not in the library,
Olga and Ivan
will not be in the library.

Now it is time for the Great Terror.
Take Tukhachevsky...
Take him and execute him.
Let the German tanks encircle Stalingrad. This
is an example of the perfective aspect
of the Russian verb.

When Vladimir Ilyich stepped off the train
at the Finland Station
a band struck up! Thousands cheered! Red-and-gold banners
flapped in the wind! It was a scene
out of a dream
dreamt by the Petersburg
League for the Liberation of the Working Class.

Seventy-five years!
Week follows week, day after day:
ponedéľnik, ftórnik, sredá, chetvérg... These are words
that bounce off the teeth. Remember,
the genitive singular of feminine nouns
is often the same
as the nominative plural.

Don't ask stupid questions.
Throw a quick glance over one shoulder, throw salt
over the other. Soon
you shall speak perfect Russian—
so flawlessly,
so fluently,
not even your comrades
will understand.

October 1992

~

During the first few years I was lucky to have as tutors a succession of native Russian speakers. Mostly they were undergraduates at the university where I was working as a carpenter. One of them was a brilliant young biochemistry student from Leningrad (St. Petersburg). He was a demanding teacher, a real taskmaster who seemed to delight in red-penciling my written exercises. On the eve of his departure for graduate school in Washington, he invited me over for a farewell dinner.

He was living for a few weeks, rent-free, in a vacated apartment. It was completely bare. With makeshift furniture and rudimentary utensils we enjoyed a carefully prepared meal. I had brought a bottle of wine, and after dinner we sat on the floor, talking. About Russia. His English was excellent.

The siege of Leningrad and the massive suffering of an entire population, the ominous quality of life under Communist rule, the experience of terror, the present complete breakdown of the economic system—all this was a far remove from the idyllic ambiance of a summer evening in a small college-town in Oregon.

At one point he asked me about my poetry: How did a poem start? I've forgotten what I replied, but driving home late that night I began composing this next poem.

MAKING DO

Two concrete blocks and a cardboard box
will serve as chairs and table.
A bare apartment needn't inconvenience you.
By all means
invite a friend. Drink wine. Converse. Discuss
the latest news
from Petersburg or Moscow.

If death is near, ask him to come—
he won't require
an extra chair. If there's no wine, water will do,
but keep the guest list small:
Vilyam Shekspir, Samu-el' Beket… and don't forget
Chekhov, of course, master
of the banal.

After the guests arrive
make sure the door is barricaded, the windows
boarded up.
This is no picnic, citizens.
Deliberately, one by one,
light the three remaining candles.
Call them by their proper names:
Faith, Hope, Charity (or is it
Clarity?).

If there are no candles, darkness will do.
Hold hands, sing songs, tell dirty jokes,
or else exchange
scientific information.

But... if words fail, silence will do. Silence
will have to do, comrades,
silence and darkness...
It will not
be as bad as you think. It will be worse
than you can imagine.

for Dmitri K.

~

In the summer of 1994 I went to St. Petersburg. For three months I boarded with a Russian family, in their large apartment on Mayakovsky Street, just four doors off Nevsky Prospekt. I studied Russian. I explored the city.

By 1994 most of the trappings of Soviet Communism had already disappeared, like so much window dressing. But traces of Lenin were still everywhere in evidence: busts and monuments, bronze and marble plaques embedded in the sides of buildings.

The Smolny Institute had been a women's boarding school in tsarist times. It was taken over by the Bolsheviks in 1917 and served as their headquarters. Momentous decisions were made here in the weeks and months following the Revolution. Lenin had his office here. Later the building was preserved as a museum, one of the hallowed places of Soviet power.

Our tour guide pointed proudly to Lenin's typewriter on a stand next to his desk. It was an Underwood! The American company must have had a franchise to produce Russian-language typewriters in pre-revolutionary Russia. I thought to myself: How strange, that the Russian Revolution should have been orchestrated on an American-brand typewriter!

LENIN'S TYPEWRITER

Sparrows and pigeons. No squirrels. Crows. A tank
on a pedestal. T-34.
Photograph this,
with the weeds overtaking the wrought-iron fence
and the shattered statue
of a Young Pioneer.
Remember,
first there was the Revolution,
then there was the War.

Defenders of Leningrad, take your positions.
One with a shovel, another a rifle—
you shall be cast in bronze.

Trash on the sidewalk along the canal.
Dogshit and broken glass.
A marble plaque commemorates
V. I. Lenin's having hidden out here once,
July of 1917.
                    And in the Smolny
is Lenin's typewriter—
squatting there like some infernal dream machine,
still spitting out in Russian letters
recipes for revolution.

Clackety-clackety-clack...

Inkstand, green felt, a gooseneck lamp
and the trusty Underwood—
what more do you need to change the world?

But those prescriptions went awry.
They're selling them on the street for souvenirs.
Come to Russia, and bring cash! Maybe
you can make a deal—
on an icon or a cathedral,
a typewriter
or a tank.

St. Petersburg
August 1994

~

Trying to grasp another language is tantalizing. It requires considerable guesswork, becoming itself an act of imagination. The museum described in the next poem is a fiction, a metaphor, a composite of the various museums I visited in Russia. The tour is a fantasy. In fact, Russian history itself is a kind of strange fairy tale or fantasy. As witness the lives of the three poets mentioned:

ALEKSANDR BLOK (1880–1921), greatest of the Russian Symbolists, is to modern Russian poetry what Rilke is to German, or Yeats to English poetry. He died soon after the Revolution, disheartened by the turn it had taken.

NIKOLAI GUMILYOV (1886–1921), traveler, adventurer, husband of Anna Akhmatova, founder of the Acmeist movement—this "Last Knight of Russia" was not allowed to attend Blok's funeral and was executed by the Bolsheviks shortly thereafter.

SERGEI YESENIN (1895–1925), a peasant's son from the Russian countryside, had a meteoric rise to fame in the years immediately preceding the Revolution. Later he was married to the American dancer Isadora Duncan, and still later hanged himself in a Leningrad hotel room after writing a last poem with his own blood.

THE MUSEUM OF RUSSIAN HISTORY

Our tour guide speaks in rapid Russian
that I can barely understand.
"This first exhibit," she explains,
"is a tableau
depicting one of our most famous Russian customs."
Blindfolded, against the wall,
comrade Stalin with his pipe
is smiling
at the firing squad.

"Very interesting!" we observe,
and go on to the next:
an enormous panorama entitled *The Defense
of Sevastópol.* In the foreground
Galina Stepanovna
(my landlady) is crouched beside a campfire,
besieged by wounded soldiers.
She's busy preparing
cabbage soup.

Then suddenly—heroic music,
sound effects... the thin, metallic voices
of the poets, Gumilyov and Blok,
barely audible
above the crash and din of Revolution.
Yesenin is there too,
a life-size wax replica in peasant costume,
passionately reciting verses
to a birch tree.

The axe, the whip, an icon;
gilded cherubs and the twisted wreckage
of the German tanks...
It's complicated, and the language
is hard to follow.
In any case, the tour is brief.
"There's more, of course," our guide assures us,
"but it
is not for foreigners."

~

One thing leads to another, and in January 1996 I returned to the former Soviet Union, this time to its southern extremity, the Crimea. I was in charge of a group of American students taking classes at Simferopol State University. I took classes, too.

The woman with whom I boarded for four months worked as a director at the local television station. One day she invited me to go along on the expedition described in the following poem. The purpose of the trip was to document on film the last days of a collective farm. The farm, with its idealized Soviet-style name, was soon to be privatized. The dreams of socialism were coming to an end.

FRIENDSHIP OF THE PEOPLES

Six empty vodka bottles on the table,
and the remnants of a feast. On the collective farm
called *Drúzhba Naródov* — Friendship
of the Peoples —
it's a holiday. The director
is Ukrainian.
His name is Peter.

There's singing, of course, and speeches;
and for the young folk
a judo tournament. The local
militia is there,
and sportsmen from the school. There's also the man
who can raise a chair above his head
with his teeth.
                    What teeth! What a neck!
— "A real animal!" says Galina
disparagingly.

Galina works for Crimean Television. We are filming
an episode in the series *How People Live*
on a collective farm.
"It's altogether different in America," I say (in Russian,
trying hard to sound casual). "There's not
such merriment,
and the vodka's not so good."

Later we tour the rice fields
in a brand-new Russian jeep. Tractors
are dragging enormous plumes of dust across the steppe,
obscuring the horizon.

Now the cameraman is shooting *us* — Peter and me —
standing on the dike, absorbed in conversation.
Peter is explaining everything.
I'm listening
intently. I can hardly
understand a word.

~

Many months after returning from the Crimea I received a letter from my landlady (in Russian, of course; she couldn't speak English) asking that I send her "the poem about our visit to the collective farm." She said that the footage of the director and me on the dike engaged in conversation was excellent. They were going to use it in the film, and also wanted to include my poem.

How did she know about the poem? I had just finished working on it the week before! It was uncanny! I must have mentioned jokingly once that someday maybe I would write such a poem... But in any case, the poem was in English—how was she going to read it? So, as an exercise, I decided to translate it. Here it is in Russian, corrected and polished with the help of my various Russian teachers. I've never seen the film.

ДРУЖБА НАРОДОВ

На столе
шесть пустых бутылок из-под водки,
и остатки банкета. Сегодня праздник
в колхозе,
который называется «Дружба народов» (Friendship
of the Peoples). Директор—
украинец.
Имя—Петр.

Здесь пение есть, конечно, и речи.
А для молодежи
турнир дзюдо. Местная
милиция присутствует,
и спортсмены из школы. Есть и мужчина,
который может зубами поднять стул
над головой.
                    Какие зубы! Какая шея!
—Настоящий зверь!—говорит Галина
неодобрительно.

Галина работает на крымском телевидении.
Мы снимаем
эпизод из серии «Как живут люди»
в колхозе.
—В Америке совсем по-другому,—говорю я (по-русски,
пытаясь звучать непринужденно).—Там
не так весело,
и водка не такая хорошая.

Позже мы объезжаем рисовые поля
на новеньком русском джипе. Трактора
тащат огромные перья пыли через степь,
затемняя горизонт.

Сейчас оператор н а с снимает — Петра и меня —
пока мы стоим на дамбе и разговарываем. Петр
объясняет все.
Я слушаю
напряженно. Я почти не понял
ни слова.

— Клеменс Старк
(перевод автора с
английского языка)

~

The Russian word *protokol* has a different sense from the corresponding English "protocol." The English word usually refers to rules prescribing etiquette and correct procedure, whereas in Russian a *protokol* (pronounced pra-ta-KOHL) is a record of proceedings, as evidence to be submitted in a court of law, or simply the minutes of a meeting. Russian also makes a verb of it: *protokolirovat'*, to "protocolize," to compile a *protokol*. Which is what the police official is doing in this next poem.

In part, the poem is a tribute to Mikhail Zoshchenko (1895–1958), the classic writer of Soviet satire. His sketches and short stories published in the '20s are comic masterpieces. His name is pronounced ZOSH-shenk-uh.

Riding the bus in a Russian city is not something easily described. The number of persons squeezed into a Russian bus at times exceeds the limits of physical probability. It is a truly collective experience.

PROTOKOL

I

I'm sitting in the police station, telling
my story.
Tat'yana is there too, helping.
Six times I tell the story, each time
to a different person,
and each time (if I may say so) the story
gets better.

I was on a trolleybus. The trolleybus was crowded.
Very crowded.
I was conscious of my body,
and of the five other bodies pressing
against mine.

I had just bought a book. Several books.
One was by Zoshchenko.
He's one of my favorite authors.

2

Now a man is writing down my story.
With a fountain pen.
At a desk that looks like it was manufactured
before the Revolution.
Or maybe just after the Revolution, at about the time
Zoshchenko
was telling his stories.

Another man is at another desk,
a cigarette in one hand.
The index finger of the other is jabbing
at a typewriter.
He's typing
someone else's story.

Tomorrow is a holiday—
Victory Day. I was on my way
to the university.
I had to wait a long time for a trolleybus.
That's why it was so crowded.

3

The man whose job it is
to write down *my* story
ponders before he writes. Each sentence
is premeditated.
His composure is almost beatific. His penmanship
is also quite remarkable.

The other man
is having trouble with his typewriter.
The carriage has jammed. *"Mashínka slomálas'!"* —
Typewriter's broke!
He pounds the desk.
He pounds the typewriter.

The room is drab and bare.
Green wallpaper. A floral pattern. Water-stained.
It looks like it too
dates from the time of Zoshchenko.

4

Finally it's my turn to write. I write
what I am told,
and I write very carefully also, because
I am writing in Russian.

Tat'yana gives me some leaves to chew.
They taste like chicory.
"*Óchen' polézni!*" she says—Very healthy!—and goes on
to inform me that what I have just written
is to affirm
that what the man has written
is correct.

And it is correct. It is my story.

5

Now the man is copying what he has written
onto a second sheet of paper.
He has that look
of a missionary, zealously translating
Paul's Epistles
into some outlandish tongue.

Otherwise, he seems like a reasonable man.
He smiles sometimes
and asks me questions.
The same questions he asked before.

I try to tell my story
as simply as I can.
I was on a trolleybus. The Number Four
trolleybus. I got on
at Lenin Square.

6

As it turns out,
there is a third sheet of paper to be inscribed
with my story. But this time
my story is abridged.
Only the important parts are told.

There's little likelihood
my wallet will be returned, the man concedes,
but still,
we have to do what we are doing—
it's protocol.

And he takes from his briefcase
another sheet of paper.
This one is not plain, however, like the others.
This one is a form to be filled out,
and at the top
is written, in Russian letters:

PROTOKOL

7

After three hours and forty minutes
we say goodbye.
I thank the man. I thank Tat'yana for her help.
And I set out, on foot,
across the boundless distances of Russia.

A metaphor, of course. In fact,
I'm walking along Kievskaya, trying not to look
like a foreigner.

Suddenly, for no reason,
I recall the story of the Peach Blossom Spring.
It's not Russian, it's an old
Chinese story.
But it's a good story.
Zoshchenko would have liked it.

Simferopol'
April 1996

~

Following my second trip to Russia, I continued my interest in and exploration of Russian culture. I learned that the earliest extant work of Russian literature is a twelfth-century epic poem called *The Song of Igor's Campaign*. It tells the story of a prince of Kievan Rus', Igor Svyatoslavich, who set out to do battle with a nomadic tribe of Turkic people encroaching on his territory. He was soundly defeated and taken captive.

I found it curious that the story of a resounding defeat serves as the Russian national epic, and wondered if that doesn't indicate something embedded deeply in the collective Russian psyche.

Some seven hundred years after Igor, my mother-in-law, as a very young Jewish girl in pre-revolutionary Russia, remembered having to hide under the bed during a pogrom.

SAVING RUSSIA

Eight hundred years ago—
eight hundred thirteen, to be exact—on a Tuesday
in April, a day like today,
Prince Igor
set out on his rash expedition
to save the Russian land.

One thing's for certain:
he never consulted my mother-in-law. She
would have told him
that Russia could not be saved.
Her family left, early in 1917, and came to Minnesota:
Elisavetgrad to Duluth
by way of China and Japan...

Igor's forces were outnumbered.
Hacking and clobbering,
the enemy horsemen crossed the Dónyets
and made mincemeat of the Russians.

Igor was captured,
but later escaped, and made his way back home.

My mother-in-law moved to San Diego,
taking with her her story
about Cossacks
and pogroms.

As a boy in upstate New York in the early 1950s, I belonged to the Ground Observer Corps. It was a branch of Civil Defense. From a rotunda atop the tallest building in Rochester, we watched for enemy planes. We all knew that if they came they would be coming from the north, sweeping down from the Arctic across Canada. They would be Russian.

At that time many people were building bomb shelters in their backyards. In school the siren would sound for an air-raid drill...

Now it was 1997. The Cold War was over. History plays some strange tricks.

EMILY CARR (1875–1941) is one of Canada's best-known and best-loved artists. Her intense and compelling nature paintings have been compared to those of Georgia O'Keeffe, Edvard Munch, and Vincent van Gogh.

FOXTROT U-521

When I was in Vancouver
I never did
see the Russian submarine,
although it was on display, open to the public
from 9:30 to 6:30 every day of the week
except Monday.

Instead
I visited the art museum—
an exhibit of paintings by Emily Carr.

The paintings were memorable;
but even without having seen it, I can picture
the submarine, a sleek
steel cigar,
probing the waters of the Pacific
with its deadly arsenal, and its crew of seventy-five...
Foxtrot U-521.
On patrol.
Engaged in secret surveillance.

All those years! The fear of imminent catastrophe!
And now the sub is docked
at a quay in New Westminster, just another
overpriced
tourist attraction.

China Basin

Away with the finery and paint of words,
which weaken
the force of what is said.

—ST. AMBROSE, BISHOP OF MILAN,
FOURTH CENTURY

For Barbara,
and for Rachel,
Daniel
and Deborah

I

Falsework

CHINA BASIN

*"Caputo's I-280 Job
Straddles Mainline"*

— *CALIFORNIA BUILDER &
ENGINEER*, OCT. 9, 1970

I

George and I work high.
Hal's the foreman. He and Deeno
rig for us
on the ground, a hundred feet below.
It's not a bridge exactly, it's a stretch
of elevated freeway
over the San Francisco rail yards—a district
called China Basin.

We're the falsework crew. Our leader
is a Cherokee from Oklahoma
everyone calls "Chink."
(Don't get the wrong idea! Chink commands respect,
from everyone.
He knows his stuff.)

Here's what we do:

A set of concrete columns
has been formed and poured, by another crew.
The columns range in height from 70
to 120 feet.
                    Around each column
we erect scaffolding,
or shoring,
made up of heavy steel pipe frames. Each frame
weighs about a ton.

The shoring cages the column
and rests
on four small pads called "sand jacks."
We stack the frames until we reach the top.

Now what we have
is a Tinkertoy tower
surrounding each column. These will support
the pair of huge steel I-beams
we gently nudge into place
(George on top of one column, I on another),
joining column to column,
spanning the tracks.

3

Our tools include
a 12-inch Crescent, a spud wrench, a straight-claw
hammer, side-cutters, and a couple
of 35-ton truck cranes.
We set everything in place with the cranes.

Cables, shackles, slings, and chokers. Chains
and chain-binders.

It's called "falsework" because
it all disappears—
it's temporary, the support system
for a massive, poured-in-place concrete beam
(called a "cap")
which will serve as underpinning
for the roadbed itself.

4

Once the cap is poured and allowed to cure,
the sand jacks are released, the forms
are stripped,
and it's our turn again.

This is the tricky part.

We delicately pluck the hundred-foot I-beams
out from under the concrete cap
with our cranes:
                              Chink is signaling the operators
down below, George and I
are crawling around like spiders up above,
rigging,
cutting the beams loose,
and everything proceeds in reverse
as we disassemble
the falsework.

And then the operation starts all over again,
on the next set of columns
along the tracks.
The job lasts a year and a half.

GANDY DANCING

Two days on Burnside was enough.
We jumped a freight,
rode it as far as Pendleton, and took the bus from there.
Paul knew a guy in Meacham
could get us work on a section gang...

Gandy dancing! Tamping ballast
under railroad ties,
compacting crushed rock and gravel, jacking up
low spots in the track
while the foreman on his knees
eyeballs the rail.

We work in pairs—two men
facing off, driving the six-foot tamping bars
with a flinging motion
into the ballast
in sync.
          "In sync," that is, unless your partner
happens to be
a squat, pudgy, out-of-sync, herky-jerky, hungover
Navajo named Charlie.

NIAGARA CYCLO-MASSAGE

Tommy Sotello and I
were selling Niagara Cyclo-Massage
at a booth we'd been assigned to, in a shopping mall
on the outskirts of San Francisco.
Tommy had bad teeth,
and he couldn't stay off the bottle.
He had quit his job as a cook,
or been fired. A few months earlier, I'd been
paid off a ship
in Oakland. We were both
making a career move.

By midafternoon
my feet hurt,
and Tommy's speech was slurred. Attempts
to lure passing shoppers into our booth for a demo
had met with little success.
Evidently the populace wasn't ready
for Niagara Cyclo-Massage.

At Monday morning sales meetings
Norm Schwartzenburg
pumped us all up like balloons. He spoke rhapsodically
of what Niagara had to offer.
But it was clear
I wouldn't be making *my* fortune here.
I thought of going back to sea,
or else marrying Barbara
and raising children...

I didn't confide in Tommy—he
was proud of his job.
"This is my office!" he'd say, with arms flung out
and a shit-faced grin,
standing at the intersection of two aisles
in a discount department store.

And looking suave
in his cheap gray suit, with the cuff links
and the pink-and-gray tie,
he'd step out onto the loading dock
for a cigarette
and a long pull on his flask.

THE GROCERY BUSINESS

First I went down to the street
by means of the stairs,
just imagine it,
by means of the stairs.

— "A BALLAD OF GOING DOWN TO
THE STORE," MIRON BIALOSZEWSKI
(TRANSLATED BY CZESLAW MILOSZ)

I

I was a cowboy once,
if you can call
a green 19-year-old from upstate New York
a cowboy.
I worked for Leo Flower. He ran cattle
on the North Fork of the John Day
in eastern Oregon.

It was straight out of the movies!
He was the local cattle baron, and I was
his young sidekick.

Some days we'd ride for miles
repairing fence, or moving cattle
from one of his ranches to another. Long hours
in the saddle,
and Leo would talk…

2

He'd been a logger, a topper. He'd fallen
over a hundred feet from the top of a Ponderosa pine
and lived,
but had to learn to walk again.
So then he became a barber.
He cut hair.
Nevada, Oregon, Idaho...

Later he worked as a timber cruiser,
made some good money,
saved it,
and bought back the family ranch.

Every month he'd give me a haircut.
And he gave me a lot of advice.

3

Evenings, in the bunkhouse, I would read.
Darwin and Freud. Santayana's *The Sense of Beauty*.
By a kerosene lamp.

According to Leo, with my
book-learning and strict, methodical approach to things,
I was ideally suited to being
a storekeeper,
and he offered to set me up in the grocery business.

However, with my limited grasp of economics,
I couldn't see
how the nearby town (Population 250)
could support a second grocery store. Besides,
it didn't fit in with my plans.

So I demurred, and eventually
moved on.

4

Years later, in San Francisco,
reading the Polish poet Bialoszewski's "Ballad
of Going Down to the Store,"
I thought about Leo
and the grocery business.

I entered a complete store;
lamps of glass were glowing.

I hardly remembered a single word
of Leo's advice.
But even now I could tell you exactly
the words of the poem.

RAINER MARIA RILKE GOES CONSTRUCTION

I try to imagine Rilke
showing up for work one morning on the construction site,
his sad, dark eyes and drooping mustache
conspicuous
under the yellow hard hat.
Not to mention the angels accompanying him.

"That's the new laborer," somebody says.
"He can't hardly speak English,"
says somebody else.
                    And then, as if on cue,
all the bosses I've ever worked for
merge
and descend on him
in a cyclone of animadversion.

Angels scatter like dandelion fluff.
Rilke is visibly shaken.

I can see the poor bastard doesn't know
which end is up, and so
I take him aside, and in a friendly way I say, "Rainer,
get your ass in gear—we got work to do!
Quit fooling with them angels!"

Or else I take another tack, back off and ask him
something technical,
like:
     "What is the sound of a jackhammer
breaking up concrete
in heaven?"

He doesn't savvy.
But later, at coffee, I ask the other laborers
how the new guy's working out,
and one of them says affably, "Not bad.
For a poet."

2

Everybody *likes* him! I can't get over it.
"He's just like one of us," the plumber foreman
tells me once.
They call him "The Dutchman,"
or just plain "Kraut,"
as in:
     "Hey, Kraut, get us some eight-foot
two-by-fours, will you?"

At night he hits the bars,
and I hear stories
how the women really go for him—his accent, his
sensitivity…

The upshot of it is, in this scenario,
Rilke goes on to great success
as a construction super.
I drop out, get steady work
fixing doors and mending broken windows—
healing
the wounds in buildings.

Now and then
I get a letter. He always asks, "What *is*
the sound of a jackhammer
breaking up concrete
in heaven?"

II

Camouflage

THE WISDOM OF CAMOUFLAGE

What did I learn in the wars?
... Above all I learned the wisdom of camouflage,
not to stand out, not to be recognized,
not to be apart from what's around me...

— YEHUDA AMICHAI (TRANSLATED BY
BARBARA AND BENJAMIN HARSHAV)

I

A telephone solicitor
calls to inquire, would I be interested in...? I can't
make out the rest—it's
unintelligible.
There's no telling what she means.

The urge to speak clearly
is overwhelming.
It obsesses me,
            as though my life depended
on correct pronunciation.

I can see myself
being led to the wall, blindfolded, hands
lashed behind my back,
and the voice of my interrogator:
"What have you learned from life?"

I can hear the click of the rifles
as the safeties are released,
and I cry out:
"Above all, I have learned the wisdom of camouflage!"

"That's plagiarism," the voice retorts,
"Yehuda Amichai said that."

It's true.
He said it first.
I know I should be more original...
But wait—
       he said it in Hebrew, I say it in English!
Doesn't *that* count for something? Besides,
Mr. Amichai
is a man worth stealing from.

3

Slouched in the cab of my Peterbilt,
disguised as the Israeli poet Yehuda Amichai,
I wait my turn in line
at the border crossing.
Exhaust fumes billow and swirl in the chill night air,
softening
the red glare of taillights.

This fake identity
fits me like a second skin. Not even I
know who I am.
               I'm traveling
under sealed orders:
destination problematical, ETA uncertain,
my cargo contraband of some sort.

To all appearances, I am nothing
if not cool. Equanimity
is my middle name.
But that's all camouflage—underneath,
I'm scared stiff. These two border guards
are eyeing me suspiciously.

I can feel
the cold stare as one of them looks up
from thumbing through my documents
and says:
          "Yehuda *who*? Why you
aren't even Jewish!"
                 Oy, it's true, it's true.
But I was married by a rabbi once,
and I have vowed
to study the Torah.

4

Strictly speaking, this is not a poem.
It doesn't rhyme, and it leaves you dangling,
undecided
whether to shit or go blind.

> (That's an expression
I've heard many times. It doesn't
make much sense,
but then, what does *making sense* mean?)

So let's get on with it. Let's
exhume the bodies,
each with a single bullet hole
through the frontal bone of the skull.

This one was disloyal, and this one was a Jew.
And this one simply
came to doubt. Oooh, *doubt!*
Strange word! Spelled with a *b.*
It should be pronounced "dowbit" or "doobit," but it's not.
It's "dowt."
And under certain circumstances
it can get you shot.

5

"Don't forget," the poet says,
"even a fist
was once an open palm with fingers."

I'm with Amichai.
If they come looking for me, you can tell them
I am nowhere to be seen. I'll blend
into the landscape,
a shepherd with a flute.

Or let them think I am a tree! Let them
mistake me
for foliage!
                And if that doesn't work
I'll make up edifying stories
to divert them,
or relate the life and wonders
of the Baal Shem Tov.

III

Deciding the Course

BASIC MANEUVERS

I was twelve. The war was over,
cutting short my dreams of glory
as a fighter pilot.
No longer could I hope
someday to sit in the cockpit of a P-38, alone
out over the Pacific,
looking for Japs to tangle with.

So I decided to become
a crop duster.
I sent away to the institute in El Paso
for the free literature,
and for months I would practice basic maneuvers,
mentally—
                    zooming in
at low altitude
in my Stearman biplane, skimming the fields, leaving behind
huge clouds of DDT,
then pulling up steeply, clearing by inches
the tops of the trees...

Later on I discovered Bashō and Issa, wonderful poems
by Takagi Kyozo—and the shakuhachi flute!
Also I read *Silent Spring*.
So it's probably just as well
my plans didn't work out.

YOKOHAMA

Wondering why not a single plum tree grew
in the holy compound of the Ise Shrine,
Bashō was told
there was no special reason...

Hot night on Isezaki Street.
Big yellow moon.
Storefront TV. After six full innings Tokyo
leads Hiroshima, 5 to 3.

What *is* this anyway? Japanese bartenders look
like American bartenders.
Sonuvabitch! Drunk in Yokohama
and Bashō isn't here.

AT SEA

"Another Christmas shot to hell,"
the bosun says. Mid-ocean, last traces of Asia
five days astern.
Door to steel locker rattles softly.
Open porthole, cold air
sucked in.

"Nothing out here
but us," the bosun says. Black lacquerware
sky, thin
sliver of the waning moon.

Course is zero-eight-zero. Following seas.

Bosun's name is McCaskey.
He's a high roller.
In the galley, over coffee and a cigarette, he discusses
women,
and the best way
of stopping off a mooring line.

WHY BUDDHISTS DON'T KILL FLIES

By actual count there are twenty-eight flies
stuck to the flypaper
dangling from a beam in the kitchen,
twenty-eight sentient beings.

Recorded live
in an auditorium far from the Himalayas,
the Gyuto monks—a Tantric choir—are chanting,
making unearthly sounds.

My wife and I are at the table
drinking coffee, listening. Our daughter's perfume
floats down the stairs,
impinging on us.

This table measures three-and-a-half foot by six.
On it are books and flowers, a basket
of tangerines. If you ask, I will say
we are happy.

And if you ask why Buddhists don't kill flies...
Figure it yourself!
Exiled monks. Twenty-eight flies.
A kitchen in Oregon. A mountain in Tibet.

TULIPS

Three yellow tulip petals
embellish the driveway. Crushed rock glistens
after the rain.
First Saturday in April. Car won't start.
This is a problem
never envisioned by Wang Wei.

After two hours spent fooling with it,
pondering at length
the intricacies of the internal combustion engine,
I emerge from under the hood,
greasy
but triumphant:
the bastard finally starts!

And then the oil filter blows.

Dropping to my knees,
with concentrated effort I observe
the puddle of cold, black oil—a little flood—
seep into the gravel,
back to the earth
whence it came.

AIRLIE ROAD

Retracing the route
of the old Applegate Trail: it crosses
a river valley, a patchwork
of tilled fields
and pasture where sheep graze, and passes through
what's left of Airlie,
the town named for a Scottish earl
a century ago.

The railroad came to Airlie once; there were
high hopes...
Two hotels, a restaurant, train station,
the general store—
all gone.
        The pavement continues,
bridging the river
at Maple Grove, another place
in name only.

Before the Europeans came, native
peoples lived here.
Dispossessed, they disappeared, leaving their name
to the river:
        Che luk i ma uke—
        Luckiamute.

To the west the Coast Range looms.
On the flanks of the mountains clear-cuts
dusted with snow...
Clouds obscure
the outline of the peaks.

I TRY TO TUNE IN CHARLES GOODRICH READING HIS POEMS OVER THE RADIO, BUT CAN ONLY GET THE BBC WORLD SERVICE, SO I LISTEN TO THE NEWS FROM ALBANIA INSTEAD

Albania is a small country.
You may not even know where it is.
In Albania
the mountains rise abruptly from the sea,
and there are many poets in Albania,
and storytellers—
like Ismail Kadaré,
whose fabulous tale *The General of the Dead Army*
I discovered once
among the trash books and assorted junk
at the Union Gospel Rescue Mission thrift store
on Commercial Street
in Salem, Oregon.

Just think of it!
The Union Gospel Rescue Mission!
A soup kitchen. A flop house. A place of overnight respite
for the homeless
and the hopeless, and here was the general
digging up his dead soldiers
in the middle of this huge, rich country blessed
beyond deserving, a long way
from Albania.

HOW TO BURY A DEAD HORSE

Call Mick Wood.
If he can't do it, call Jim King.
Then call your boss and tell him
you'll be late for work, you've got to
bury a dead horse.
Take your chainsaw. Clear a path through the woods
for the backhoe.

Suppose you were a horse—an Arabian, say,
a golden palomino—
and you knew that it was time to die.
What would you do? Where
would you go?

Sprawled out in the grass,
in a meadow,
on the first warm day of spring . . .

Let the vultures peck out her eyes.
Let the coyotes rip her throat.
She's lived her life.
She's gone.
        Call the kids and tell them
Shur-reka's dead.

WHAT TO SAY
TO YOUR NEUROSURGEON

"Maurice" let's call him. And so
you'll say, "Maurice,
I know a traveler's legs are often weary,
but this pain in mine…"
When he starts talking bone scan, MRI, stenosis, laminectomy,
pretend that you're a simpleton. Don't let him know
you know
a thing or two yourself.

Ask him how much he makes
an hour. Remind him to make sure his tools are sharp
before he carves you up.

Be philosophical. As Ouspensky said, "Life
is a pain factory."

LINGUISTICS

Poems in Russian and Portuguese, thousands
in Chinese alone,
each language its own little system of sounds
for the mouth to master...
A glutton, I aspire to mouth them all,
but never will,
pushing sixty.

To console myself, I make up a few sounds of my own,
walking back to the house
after midnight, night sky
pricked with stars, a complete moon
glowing.

If only I had wised up sooner! I might have achieved
enlightenment by now,
or at least have learned how to conjugate
the irregular verbs
in Hungarian, say.

DECIDING THE COURSE
MY EDUCATION SHOULD TAKE

Maybe I already know
as much as I'm destined to know, for this lifetime,
about small-engine repair.
And also about plumbing.
For that matter, I wouldn't mind
drinking a beer
to celebrate
an end to plumbing, and an end to small-engine repair.

Why not study ethnobotany,
or practice juggling?
I could learn to read Chinese, and start in
on the ten thousand poems extant
of Lu You.

It's unlikely I'll take up blacksmithing,
or become a backhoe operator.

For the time being
I think I'll just concentrate
on finding the words
for the mist that rises from the fields in the morning,
or the moon
as seen once from Joel's truck
on the way home from a job in Corvallis.

Traveling Incognito

I

LOOKING FOR WORK: SEVEN POEMS
INSTEAD OF A RESUMÉ

1. *The Plan*

My plan was simple.
I'd go to some remote, exotic place
like Kansas City,
and get a job, any job—pumping gas or
scraping hash browns from the grill in a sleazy diner.
I'd rent a furnished room
in a rundown neighborhood, and there, evenings
and on my days off, I'd be free
to study and to read, to continue
my education.
     I'd start working on a novel,
and maybe meet a girl...
It would be enough. It would be a life,
a living.

2. *Digging Footings*

Sparky's the sawyer.
He's only got three fingers on one hand.
Big belly. Thick neck. A pencil stub
behind his ear. Nobody
messes with Sparky.
                          I'm his helper, I pack lumber
to and from the saw, keeping
the carpenters supplied.
Before that, I worked with Vince and Otto,
digging footings.

No backhoes on this job, it's strictly
a pick-and-shovel show—
twenty of us laborers strung out across the site,
all elbows and assholes.

Vince is short and skinny. He's Italian. Otto's a German,
short and fat. Just trying to keep up with them
takes all I've got.
But hey,
it's summer, I'm 18, and union scale
is two-sixty-four an hour.

3. *Union Pacific*

Foreman's name is Ferdinand—
Ferdinand Thyfault.
We just call him "TEE-foe."
He's French-Canadian, from Kansas, one of those
old-time railroad men. He bleeds
Union Pacific.
     Our job is to maintain
the Duncan section,
an isolated twenty-mile stretch
of U.P. mainline
winding through a canyon carved by Meacham Creek
on the western slope of the Blue Mountains
in northeast Oregon.

The crew is a congenial bunch
of misfits and losers—some local types, a kid my age
from east Texas, an Arkie, a Swede, a couple
of Navajos...

Sometimes I write love letters for Herbert Sandoval
to his girl
back on the reservation.
"Listening to the wind in the pines," I write,
"I think of you."
"Okay," Herbert says, "that's
pretty good."

4. *Mariposa Slim*

The first I ever heard
of Mariposa Slim, that legendary railroad bull,
was in a hobo jungle outside Yuma
from a 'bo whose name I can't remember,
but do remember
how he liked to quote passages from Shakespeare
followed by the attribution
"Snakeshit."

He and I teamed up together
for the ride to Indio—a most unlikely
pair of travelers.

He used to make his living breaking horses, he said.
He also said he served on submarines once
in the war.
        Well, maybe, maybe not—with guys like that
it's hard to tell.

5. *Eastern Shockcrete*

A precast concrete plant in rural New Jersey.
It's January. We're casting
architectural beams and columns
for a new library
in Philadelphia.

To move the columns around the yard
we use a forklift as a crane.
The carriage is run to the top of the mast,
and from the forks
a column is suspended—five tons of precast concrete
dangling like a giant pendulum.
Two of us walk close on either side to steady it
as the forklift
lurches slowly over frozen, rutted ground
to where the column
will be loaded on a flatbed.

When one of the front tires
caught my heel,
it threw me forwards, facedown, pinning me to the ground,
and continued to travel
up the back of my leg to the crotch.

Forty years later,
I can still
hear myself scream, "Back up! Back up!"

6. Oil, Paint, and Drug Reporter

Not for nothing
does the masthead read:
The Chemicals Market Authority.
It's the bible of the industry, I'm told
when I'm hired.
My job is to turn out each week a column called
"Petroleum Derivatives."
Five other reporters write columns too.
Art Kavaler is editor.

My sources of inspiration
are both numerous and reliable — Shell Oil, Monsanto,
Allied Chemical...
In my Rolodex are names and telephone numbers
compiled by my predecessors.

Although I feel like an impostor
in this ill-fitting, hand-me-down blue serge suit
given me by my wife's rich lawyer uncle,
I'm never questioned,
not even
when sneaking off to Battery Park, to sit on a bench
composing poems
about saints and demonology.

7. *The Trade*

"I'm a carpenter apprentice
looking for work," I say repeatedly,
as I crisscross the city, driving
from construction site to construction site,
trying to catch on.

First-year apprenticeship is concrete form construction.
Second-year is framing.
Evening classes. A four-year
course of study.

It's one of those halcyon days in February
in San Francisco.
I'm working my first job
as an apprentice. I'm on a scaffold
thirty feet in the air, nailing
cedar bevel siding.
                    Suddenly, looking up, I see
over the rooftops and tangle of power lines,
against a blue sky,
the Golden Gate Bridge.

It's a sight so beautiful I'm stunned.
"Jesus," I say to myself, "I've got poems in my head
and a hammer in my hand. I can't believe
they're actually paying me
to be here."

NEW ORLEANS, 1958

The way he had it figured
there were two kinds of men: cake-eaters
and world-travelers...
A traveler named Alton Parker Dahill
told me this
in a greasy spoon we both frequented, a hangout
for itinerants, on Camp Street.

Alton had a theory—it had to do with
chromosomes...
He expounded it at length.
And when he could afford the postage he would send
postcards to famous geneticists,
explaining to them
just where they had gone wrong.

It snowed that winter in New Orleans.
First time in sixty years.
When spring came, we rode the trains together
as far as Houston.
He got off. I went on. I was traveling
incognito,
developing a theory of my own.

NEVADA CITY, CALIFORNIA

The closest I ever came
to Nevada City, California,
was on a freight train out of Roseville, headed east
over the mountains.

We were stopped on a siding
to allow a westbound freight the right-of-way.
It was March. I was doing
jumping jacks
to keep warm, on the back of a flatcar I'd been riding
since Roseville—a load of steel culvert
big enough to crawl into
and hunker down, out of sight.

A brakeman, making his way along the string of cars
from the caboose, saw me
exercising.
          "Kid," he said,
"it's snowing up ahead.
You won't *make* it, unless you get your ass
into an empty boxcar."

I did what he said. He was right.
We were three days
in the mountains, Roseville to Sparks, Nevada,
with long stretches in tunnels
and on sidings,
while snowplows cleared the track.

THE *PAN-OCEANIC FAITH*

The night the *Pan-Oceanic Faith* went down
in a storm in the North Pacific,
we were a hundred miles south of her,
another freighter
plowing through stormy seas.

As it turned out,
she was a sister ship—SIU, like us. Two of our crew
had boarded her in Seattle, months earlier.
But something about her
spooked them,
and before she sailed they signed off.

The sea that night was wild—green water
breaking over our bow.
I had just been relieved at the wheel
when Sparks
stepped into the wheelhouse to report to the mate
that he'd picked up
an SOS...

When Conrad wrote, "The sea came at us
like a madman with an axe,"
he had it right.
Ten thousand tons of welded steel plate—buckled
and smashed, by water.

Three survivors, out of a crew of forty-two—
a messman,
the chief engineer, and one AB...

"Why those three?" we wondered
all the rest of the way in to Newport, Oregon,
and looked around
uneasily,
          weighing our chances,
sizing each other up.

ON THE HOOK IN MANILA

Riding at anchor in Manila Bay
after ten days at sea, watching the moon rise
over the city sparkling below,
the four of us
—Mike the oiler, Jake, and crazy Bob and I,
a scruffy bunch—
are at the rail, midships,
waiting for a launch to take us ashore.

Although in no way
could we be said to resemble
the Four Celestial Worthies, much less
the equally venerable Four Perfected Lords of Wu,
the four of us
gaze shoreward, half convinced
that every bar girl on the waterfront
will find us irresistible.

LEAVING LOS ANGELES

Once, flying out of L.A.,
having just visited my brother-in-law
who was dying of cancer,
I looked down
as the plane banked after takeoff, and I saw
that the city spread out below
was itself in fact
a cancer,
        clear evidence, it seemed,
of a disease
infecting the earth.

Observers from another planet,
or time-lapse photography
taken from such an altitude over the period, say,
of ten thousand years—the ten thousand years
just past—
would verify this.

But by the time we landed in Portland
I had other things on my mind—
the drive home, something to eat, a poem,
a good night's sleep...

II

ONE OF THE LOCALS

Summer vacations, traveling with the family,
what bothered me
was being a tourist—I didn't like
being conspicuous, I wanted
to pass as one of the locals, to speak the local dialect
with no trace of an accent. Invisibility
was my ideal.
My secret ambition—to be a spy.

In fantasy, I would parachute
behind enemy lines,
and then—disguised, let's say, as the shy, unobtrusive
village chimney sweep—
engage in daring acts of sabotage.
Later, while being awarded the *Croix de guerre*,
I would modestly downplay my exploits,
crediting
my fallen comrades.

As a matter of fact, my career in espionage
never really got off the ground,
although in practising for it I learned
to be circumspect,
and of course to be always careful
in everything I say.

DRIVING 99W, REFLECTING ON WAR
AND SOLID WASTE DISPOSAL

On 99W, about halfway
between Lewisburg and Suver Junction,
I pull over sometimes to read
the historical markers that commemorate
Camp Adair:
"Site of the cantonment
where these four infantry divisions trained for combat
in World War II..."

Across the highway
is Coffin Butte, the local landfill.
Every day
trucks and trailers from three counties converge
to deposit refuse—thousands of tons of solid waste
pushed into shape by bulldozers,   .
and overlaid with glistening black plastic,
as though it were
a preservation site.

So maybe someday what they'll say is: Once
there was a war here,
and this is where the victors
stockpiled
their plunder.

LOG TRUCKS AND COYOTES

From an upstairs window
you can hear log trucks a mile away
downshifting
for the stop sign at the Falls City junction;
and from the same window, at night sometimes,
the coyotes begin
yelping and yipping and howling,
signaling to each other.

For years I've listened to this.
My children must have listened too.

They may not know it,
but even should they live to be a hundred,
somewhere in them will be imprinted
coyotes howling,
and log trucks approaching the Falls City junction.

ANOTHER POEM ABOUT PLUMBING

When I installed this system
twenty-five years ago,
I didn't know of the difference between
Type M and Type L
copper pipe, not to mention the obvious merits
of CPVC.
        But had I known what I know now,
I wouldn't be crawling
under this house, cursing, with nothing to show
but pinhole leaks and another poem
about plumbing.

WHY THE OLD CARPENTER
CAN'T QUITE MAKE OUT
WHAT EXACTLY IS BEING SAID

Loss of hearing might account for it.
Too many hours with power tools. Too many passes
with a Skilsaw
through sheets of plywood.
Not the clangor of a gong, but the deep rattle
of a compressor.
Chipping guns and rotohammers.
Too much machinery. Too much noise.

Strange occupation for a bookworm, eh?—someone
more likely to be found
studying etymologies, and diagramming complex sentences
in languages like Old Church Slavonic
or Phrygian.
The study of grammar, it's been said, is akin
to the deepest metaphysics.

But this wood butcher is no philosopher,
unless you count
cogitating, while pounding nails, for thirty years.
He's pretty cocky for an old fart though.
When anybody on the job
praises him for his handiwork,
he replies:
            "Hey, I didn't just ride into town
on a wagonload of cabbages."

A BRIEF LECTURE ON
DOOR CLOSERS

Although heretofore unconsidered
in verse or in song,
the ordinary door closer is, I submit, a device
well worth considering.
Consisting primarily
of a spring and a piston, in combination,
here's how it works:
                    You open a door,
either pushing or pulling.
The spring is compressed, the piston extended.
Now, having passed through the doorway,
you relinquish control,
and the door closer takes over. The spring remembers
how it was—
it wants to return. But the urge is damped
by the resistance the piston encounters,
snug in its cylinder
filled with hydraulic fluid.

Such is the mechanism of the door closer,
invented in 1876
by Charles Norton, when a slamming door
in a courtroom in Cincinnati
repeatedly disrupted
the administration of justice.

· · · · ·

Whether concealed beneath the threshold
or overhead in the head jamb,
whether surface-mounted as a parallel-arm installation
or as a regular-arm,
door closers are ever vigilant,

silently performing their function, rarely
complaining.

Whereas doors can be metaphorical—as in
for example, "He could never unlock
the door to her heart"—
door closers cannot.

Remember this when you
pass through, and the door closes behind you
with a soft thud
and final click
as the latchbolt engages the strike.

THE CHINESE WAY

In reply to Master Boyce
after receiving copies of
his recent paintings

Now that you've taken to holding the brush
the Chinese way,
even Su Shi himself would pause
to admire your watercolors.

Brush strokes as simple
and as complex
as the tangle of weeds at the edge of a field,
colors as vivid as the wash is pale...

Of a friend, Su Shi said:
"When he painted bamboo
he became the bamboo, forgetting himself
as a man."

So!... Playing with your paint box,
and traveling again!
Your backpack weighs 32 pounds, you say.
Maybe by now you're in Fernie.

ON MY WAY TO WORK I PASS
BUD'S AUTO WRECKING AND
THINK ABOUT SU DONGPO

A '60s Volvo ("PARTS CAR")
rusting in the weeds by a chain-link fence
in front of Bud's Auto Wrecking
is not something you'd expect to find
in a Song dynasty
landscape painting.

But... if Su Dongpo should happen by,
he'd probably
look it over. In fact,
that small figure in the foreground
crossing a footbridge at the bottom of a steep ravine,
with craggy precipices towering over him,
looks like Su Dongpo.

The pathway leads to a pavilion
perched high among the rocks. Streamers of mist
partly obscure
the solitary traveler.

Wait a minute! That's not Su Dongpo,
it's me—stumbling along
with my toolbox and an instruction manual,
a funny-looking, bald-headed old geezer who doesn't
really need
parts for a Volvo, although
you never know...

ON THE EVE OF RETIREMENT
I HAVE THIS DREAM ABOUT
GOING BACK TO WORK

In this dream I'm hired
as a sheetmetal worker, a tin-bender
installing gutter
along the overhanging cornice of a high-rise
hundreds of feet above the street.

Although I'm inexperienced
and terrified, I know the trick
is to lay out properly, in two dimensions
on a flat surface,
what will—by cutting, bending, and crimping—
be transformed
into something three-dimensional.

Not unlike a poem, I think, as I discuss
with George Kotlarek
a particularly intricate detail, and remember
I won't get paid
till the end of the month.

A LESSON IN PHYSICS

One by one the old barns are collapsing.
Just last week one went down
on the Peoria road.
You couldn't say
it was unexpected, racked as it was and leaning
a little more out of plumb
each time I passed.

I'm closing in
on 65 myself. And although
I've been partially rebuilt, with certain adjustments
to my anatomy,
I won't last long.

A new roof and some cross-bracing
would have bought that old barn a few more years.
Triangulation
makes a difference. But in the end, gravity
takes over. Which is why
levity is so precious
while it lasts.

Rembrandt, Chainsaw

If you can make a poem
a farmer finds useful,
you should be happy.
A blacksmith you can never figure out.
The worst to please is a carpenter.

— OLAV H. HAUGE (TRANSLATED
FROM THE NORWEGIAN
BY ROBERT HEDIN)

NEIGHBORS

New neighbors
building a house up on the hill...
She raises goats. He works at the pen.
From my back door
it's thirty miles, as the crow flies,
over the mountains to the coast. It used to be
I could imagine
walking it—unimpeded.
No fences. Nothing but deer trails and logging roads.

Now I'm surrounded by neighbors.

Which is better: seeking the recluse
in the mountains, and finding he's not at home,
or helping the goat-lady
rig up a new wooden pedestal
for our mailboxes?

BUILDING SCAFFOLD

"This is how we built scaffold,"
the old-timer says, driving a screw with his cordless drill,
"except
we didn't use screws or cordless drills."

Things change. Hardly a carpenter nowadays
uses a handsaw. The folding rule
has gone the way of the dodo, and even hammers
may soon be relegated
to Antiques & Collectibles.

A scaffold, however,
is temporary by definition, a minimal structure
intended to be torn down,
a kind of medieval siege tower, or a makeshift platform
from which to contemplate
impermanence.

As the old-timer says, "It will put you in places
where no one has ever been."

THE GIRL FROM PANAMA

I'm talking with Mike over coffee.
His wife recently left him. He's lonely.
We're both carpenters, a couple of old guys in baseball caps
plying the trade.
We can frame a wall and hang a door, we can
read a set of blueprints.
But when it comes to women...

I'm thinking about my mother, who is 91
and very frail. I'm thinking
about my wife, my daughters, my granddaughter,
my sister, old girlfriends, my ex-wife,
and the girl from Panama
in the reading room of the New Orleans public library
forty-five years ago
who slipped a note to me across the table, asking:
"Are you a philosophy?"

Rain splatters against the storefront
of the coffee shop. Mike and I are silent
for a long time
before going back to work.

GADSKY, ELK-HUNTING

In the checkout line at Safeway
I run into Gadsky,
a guy I worked with once, on a job somewhere
in Woodburn or McMinnville. So we exchange a little
manly bullshit, then Gadsky begins
bending my ear
with an account of his elk-hunting exploits.

Halfway across the parking lot,
about when we get
to where Gadsky is crouching in the salal, having just spotted
a six- or seven-point bull,
my attention lapses.
                    I drift... and imagine myself
in a coffeehouse in Caracas,
where a gaggle of bearded poets
argues vociferously
over just what it is that distinguishes verse
from prose.

But what job *did* I work on
with Gadsky?
Well, whatever it was, Gadsky and I have it in common.
It distinguishes us.

IT COULD BE WORSE

Call it *sleet* or call it *snow*,
it's coming down so hard it's hard to see
the two linemen
up there at the crossarm of the pole.
They're working from the bucket of their boom truck
with come-alongs and tackle,
to retrieve our downed power lines
and re-attach us to the grid.

Four days without power
after an early winter storm savaged the countryside...
Out all day with a chainsaw
clearing limbs and broken trees from the right-of-way,
I'm standing in the snow now with the line crew foreman,
peering up,
remembering days like this on a construction site
when I wished I'd become a librarian.

It's cold. It's getting dark. I'm soaking wet. The sleet
has turned to freezing rain.
"Some fucking weather!" I say to the guy
over the roar of the truck's diesel,
and he replies: "It could be worse. You could be
sitting at a fucking desk
eight hours a day, five days a week."

MAINTENANCE & REPAIR

I'm showing the new guy
how to replace the spring-loaded pressure shoes
on an aluminum hopper window.
It doesn't require
an engineering degree, but like a lot of other simple things
—tying your shoelaces, for example,
or marriage—it's tricky.

This is my last week of work
before retiring. *I'm* being replaced. Maintenance & Repair
will continue without me.
Every day, minute by minute, things are wearing out
and breaking down.
Window hardware and body parts.
Language itself.

I'm rehearsing the speech I plan to give
at my retirement party.
"Boys," I'll say to my trusty confrères, "remember—
adjusting the spring tension
on one or the other (or both) of the nylon pressure shoes
is essential
to proper operation."

THREE SEA STORIES

1. *On a Freighter, Leaving Newport*

Thirty-seven degrees
on the inclinometer! Crossing the bar,
that old Victory ship rolled so far over on her side
the pilot, a portly man
climbing down a rope ladder
to the launch that would take him ashore,
looked like a crab
scuttling backwards, a tiny figure
on a huge teeter-totter.

But the ship righted itself, the pilot
leaped aboard his launch,
and we proceeded south along the coast, a thousand miles,
Yaquina Bay to Port Hueneme,
to top off our cargo
before heading out again, across open water,
to the war in Southeast Asia.

2. *Saga of the* Goodwill

Fore-and-aft rigged,
a two-masted schooner. Overall length: 161 feet.
Built in the '20s as a private yacht.
Largest fore-and-aft-rigged sailing vessel
in the world, we were told,
in 1968.

A group of us, as part of
a lunatic scheme,
had made an offer to purchase her.
We knew next to nothing about sailing, but planned
to make seamanship
a kind of spiritual discipline.

After a nearly disastrous
trial voyage
from Honolulu to San Francisco,
we had her hauled out for inspection. It turned out
that the steel hull
was so badly rusted in places
you could almost poke a screwdriver through it.

So the deal was off, and six months later,
when she went down with all hands
in a storm off Ensenada,
we were not aboard.

3. *On the Beach*

"I'll go to sea no more"
is what I'm thinking,
remembering the words of the song
while listening to waves crash on the beach.

I'm in a motel on the Oregon coast.
It's midnight. Full moon. January
of my 66th year.

The way the song goes,
a man, his son, and a hired hand
set out for the Grand Banks to fish for cod
in a boat built by the man's father.

What it was she struck they never knew,
but suddenly
"every seam poured water."

I've been to sea, I have a son,
and you could say
my life is a boat built by my father.

TWO PHOTOGRAPHS

In this group photograph
I'm standing—back row, center,
one of a gang of eleven young orangutans
in identical T-shirts
reading "Seafarers International Union, AFL-CIO."
A sign in the foreground:
"Lifeboat Certification Class, 1967."

For over a week, every morning
we've been rowing a lifeboat
back and forth on the icy waters of Sheepshead Bay,
preparing ourselves
to qualify
as Able-Bodied Seamen.

Another photograph
showing what could be the Lifeboat Class
thirty years later—a bunch
of amiable, aging, overweight apes—is actually
the maintenance crew
at a large university. I'm on the left,
standing, facing the camera.

A FEW WORDS ABOUT HOPE —
AND BASEBALL

Still one more month of hope
for Red Sox fans, as the Sox head back to Boston,
trailing the Yankees
by 3½ games.

"Hope" is also
the name of a town in B.C.
where I rendezvoused once with my wife and kids
while scouting the Interior,
looking around for a place to spend
the rest of our lives.

According to Paul
in one of his letters to the Corinthians, hope
"abideth."
More than that, he doesn't say.

By definition, loss of hope is desperation or despair.

In any case, I'm sitting here at the kitchen table
reading the sports section —
checking the standings, studying
the box scores.

HITCHHIKING

I was standing by the side of the road
somewhere in Idaho,
thumbing a ride. I was headed back East.
From the map I could see that the shortest way
lay through Wyoming.

Hitchhiking was my magic carpet, but it required
perseverance—and luck.
What to do next? I wondered, while pondering
schemes that involved Argentina
or Iceland,
and a system for playing the horses...

Traffic was sparse, and no car stopped.
So after four hours I quit, walked back across town,
started thumbing again—
south this time, toward Utah.

OTHERWISE

Stopping off at the Dari Mart in Harrisburg
for a six-pack of PBR,
I reflect on the path my life might have taken,
had the conjunction of planets
been otherwise.
            All things considered, I could have been
the founder of a U-Bake Pizza empire,
or wound up
living with a ditzy blonde and her two kids
in a trailer park
outside Harrisburg.

POLITICIAN IN A COWBOY HAT

No matter how bestial it may be, evil
always has a human face.

—RUSSIAN SAYING

The heavily jowled, mustachioed man
in a cowboy hat, running for county commissioner,
is an entrepreneur—
he's all business.
It may be going too far to say
if the price were right
he'd sell his own mother to the local butcher for dogfood,
but it's not unthinkable.

And while it's true
that none of the paintings of Hieronymus Bosch
actually depicts
a politician in a cowboy hat,
certain of Bosch's fantastic creatures—hoofed and feathered,
with tusks or talons—
bear a striking resemblance
to our local politico.

However, in an election year
the candidates all look alike, palavering
and preening
in front of the camera, hedging their bets on what will win
the approval of the electorate.
Read the signs:
Hewitt Can Do It. Propes Knows the Ropes.
Vote So-and-so for County Commissioner.

ECHOCARDIOGRAM

With electrodes attached to my chest,
and wires that lead
to a large apparatus resembling a pinball machine,
my heart is being monitored.
I'm watching it beat, on a computer screen.

At the same time,
I'm thinking about my old Chevy pickup—forty-eight years
since it rolled off the assembly line.
I'm exactly
twenty years older than that. No wonder
the valves are worn.

The kid who's handling the equipment is called
an "echo-tech." He learned how to do it at school
in Spokane.

·····

With my "golden years" in jeopardy,
it's time to ask some questions!
What do you make
of those old Bolsheviks
who confessed to crimes they never committed?

Or how about
the Wannsee Conference,
where finishing touches were put to the Final Solution?
What about global warming?

CAMBER

Observing the underside of freeway overpasses
is one way to kill time
on the interstate
between Portland and Seattle.
You don't have to have worked
heavy construction,
but if you have you know the lingo:

Columns, cap, and spandrel beams.
Abutments. Soffit. Cold joint. Barrier rail.

Architecturally,
even your most imposing freeway overpass
is not in the same league
with the flying buttresses of a Gothic cathedral. Still,
there is something to be said for functional
simplicity, the subtlety and grace
of camber.

ROYAL EXPRESS

"Royal Express," a blue and gold Peterbilt
out of Fresno, accelerates
and pulls out to pass
another eighteen-wheeler. All along Interstate 84
the wheels of commerce are rolling.

The truck drivers
emerging at irregular intervals from the men's toilet
in a freeway rest area west of Pendleton
are not unlike
the woodchoppers of Nishiyama
crossing the river on their way to work,
in the ancient Japanese poem.

Bearded, clean-shaven, big-bellied, skinny—the truckers
climb into their rigs.
Stacked up like logs in a mill pond:
Peterbilts, Kenworths, and Freightliners.
Volvos and Macks.

It's commerce. It's commercial,
the transport of goods in North America
and the deforestation
of Japan.

IMMORTALITY

In the one-hundred block of Twelfth Street
near the corner of Jackson,
impressed in the sidewalk—
a name and a date:

W. S. BURNAP

1917

What's there to say about Burnap,
whose legacy
is a section of sidewalk he formed and poured
on a backstreet in Corvallis
ninety-one years ago?

Burnap? Sure,
I knew him, worked with him once: a real son of a bitch.
Saturday night at the Elks
we'd tie one on
and he'd get mean, mad-dog mean.

Or maybe that's not true... Maybe
he was a pussy cat—
upstanding citizen, family man, church on Sunday,
and always with that peculiar urge
to be remembered.
                    Like another W. S.,
the poet Walter Savage Landor,
who, to ensure that his poems would last,
translated them into Latin,
as if to impress them
in concrete.

Well, anyway, if you're walking Twelfth Street
near the corner of Jackson,
gaze down at the inscription:

W. S. BURNAP

1917

and as you continue on your way
step lightly, friend, step
lightly.

KEATS AND SHELLEY

Keats and Shelley. Shelley and Keats.
Could be the name
of an insurance agency,
or a partnership of corporate tax attorneys.

But no, it's just a couple of Brits who wrote poems
a few hundred years ago.
Tenured now
in the English Department of every university,
they're resting on their laurels.

Once, triumphantly, they hurled their verses at the sky,
measured each word,
and stopped the lines with rhymes.

Immortal poets, those two—although
you wouldn't know it
to talk with Ernie. He says,
                                    "Keats and Shelley?
You mean *Sheets & Kelly*. Used to be
a plumbing contractor
in Springfield."

AN INTRODUCTION
TO RUSSIAN GRAMMAR

When it comes to the rules
for forming the *past passive participle*
of both first- and second-conjugation verbs, in Russian,
I can't help but think of Osip Emilievich,

who could take the past passive participle — among other
grammatical niceties —
and brandish it like a lion-tamer cracking his whip,
as casually as thumbing his nose.

And speaking of Mandelstam reminds me of Tsvetaeva,
who was giddy with Poetry,
and having foolishly returned to Russia in 1939,
a few years later, hopeless, hanged herself...

not long after Mandelstam had been
arrested, deported, and transformed into a mangy dog
scavenging garbage
at a transit camp in Siberia.

for V.F. and S.S.

A REPORT FROM THE PROVINCES

The flag at half-mast in front of the courthouse
probably means
another dead soldier,
or else the President has been assassinated,
which I remember happening once.

The sudden sight of the National Guard
in combat boots and camouflage
deploying briskly to military vehicles outside the armory
a block off Main Street
is not encouraging.

But I take heart
from the bumper sticker
affixed to the rear of a battered blue pickup
diagonally parked across from the post office,
which reads:
>   IF IGNORANCE IS BLISS,
>   WHY ISN'T EVERYONE HAPPY?

Dallas, Oregon
August 2006

THUCYDIDES, BILL O'REILLY AND I
DISCUSS FOREIGN AFFAIRS

O'Reilly is bad-mouthing the French
while Thucydides
recites in Greek key passages
from his monumental *History of the Peloponnesian War.*

I myself, given the bellicose nature
of certain local "patriots"
and the woeful politics of the country at large,
am simply
trying to be reasonable.

"I've been to France," O'Reilly says, "it's beautiful, very
historical."

Struck by this dim-witted observation,
I reply: "O'Reilly, I wish I could say this in Greek,
but in plain English,
you have your head up your ass."

Meanwhile, Thucydides is busy explaining
how after arriving too late to relieve the garrison
at Amphipolis,
he was relieved of his command, and so
took up writing instead.

THE GREAT BOOKS REVISITED

We were on campus
trying to bilk unsuspecting college students
out of their meager allowances. We were selling
a complete set
of handsomely bound volumes called *The Great Books*.
Erasmus was in it, and Thomas Aquinas.
Plato, of course. And others.
It was available now for only pennies per day.

My partner in this enterprise
was a gunrunner named Harry Pharr. In a previous lifetime
Harry had made a fortune
trading Winchesters and whiskey to the Indians.
But the girls of Sigma Kappa Phi
were not taken in by our scam, and we were urged
by the local constabulary
to leave town. Pronto.

My old Jaguar XK-120 roadster
was our getaway car.
It had cachet, but was short on comfort. So,
with windshield wipers flailing wildly in a torrential downpour,
ragtop flapping,
and Harry huddled shivering in the passenger seat
cursing Providence
and my choice of vehicles,

we returned to headquarters in San Francisco,
driving all night down 101
through the redwoods in the rain.

A LITTLE MEDITATION
ON MACHINES

A broken-down backhoe,
one flat tire and its bucket missing,
left in a ditch by the side of the road...
Another machine has bit the dust. Another example
of mechanical infidelity.

Although machines
are not sentient beings, like ground squirrels
or congressmen,
they have a life of their own, parallel to ours.
They can remain very quiet for a long time, gathering force,
preparing themselves
for the day they will betray us.

And although we consider ourselves superior,
compared to machines
we are nothing but small, pathetic, soft-boiled creatures
with little to brag about.

Of course there is always our famous
opposable thumb,
which enables us to play the guitar, and also
to manipulate with only one hand
the keypad on a cell phone.

THE AUTHENTICITY OF THE QUR'AN

The authenticity of the Qur'an
is proved, says Borges,
by the fact there is no mention in it
of camels — camels
being so commonplace at the time of the Prophet
their presence was taken for granted.

Whereas, had the Qur'an been composed
by a latter-day forger,
he almost certainly would have stocked it with camels,
to authenticate it.

By the same token,
the authenticity of my poems may be inferred
from the complete absence in them
of box-elder bugs.

As everyone knows,
the world consists of ten thousand things.
Mountains and rivers come first,
of course,
but also included
are baseball, box-elder bugs, and the intercontinental
ballistic missile.

It goes without saying
that after the last of the ten thousand things
there will be
the absence of things,
                            thus proving
the existence of the world.

LATE OCTOBER

I'm thinking about Rembrandt
while filing a chainsaw
that used to belong to my neighbor Lloyd Cooley,
a Stihl 017
I got at the yard sale after Lloyd died.

I'm thinking how Rembrandt
over the course of his lifetime created
nearly a hundred self-portraits, and also I'm thinking
how one of those pictures
of everyday life in Holland in the seventeenth century
might include
a carpenter in his workshop filing a saw.
Some things don't change.

It's late October. Time to reconsider
everything. With each stroke of the file I can feel
steel biting steel,
leaving each tooth with a razor-sharp edge.

Old Dogs, New Tricks

For the Queen
with a cloud
of snow-white hair

SANSKRIT

At 72, still nursing hopes
of someday living the life of a scholar,
I'm in the garage
working on my pickup again.
A bolt in the parking brake linkage has sheared.
Replacing it should've been easy, but it's turned out
to be a bitch.

At one time I thought of studying Sanskrit,
but got sidetracked
and hitchhiked south instead, looking
for adventure. I was 19.

When a knife fight broke out in a waterfront bar in Mobile,
I had to think fast.

I got out while I could, out the back
past the Men's Room, by the dumpsters in the alley,
and thence through a bleak industrial district
to my shabby furnished room,
once the parlor
of an elegant town house,

there to delve into the thirty-two volumes
of William Faulkner
for which I had ransacked used-book stores in New York
and transported
along with a sleeping bag and a toothbrush
on my way, so I thought, to a life
of scholarship and adventure.

LOOKING FOR A SHIP

I always wanted to go to sea,
Melville and Conrad were two of my heroes,
and at 19, cocky, having just dropped out of school,
I set out to do it.

By greasing the palm
of a union official in Mobile, I managed to obtain
seaman's papers
from the Coast Guard, and I hitchhiked to New Orleans
to start looking for a ship.

Living was cheap there
on skid row in 1958. Seven dollars a week
for a room not much larger than the bed it contained,
a table and chair. For only a quarter you could get
a plate of rice and beans
at Fred's Inn,
a cup of chicory coffee for a nickel.

Fred's Inn was where I learned
to differentiate
a tramp or a hobo from a bum, and where I met
characters I'd only read about in books. It was a long way
from the Ivy League.

Every day I'd navigate the waterfront,
scouting the docks, boarding every ship in sight,
trying to hire on.

But shipping was slow in the Gulf ports that winter.
With so many seamen on the beach
looking to ship out,
I didn't stand a chance.

So after a month or more I finally gave up,
packed my gear, and rode the freight trains west
to California
to see what would happen there.

. . . . .

Not until ten years later,
after a marriage and a divorce,
while another war in the Far East was heating up,
did I feel again the urge to go to sea.

I still had my papers. I knew the protocol.
I signed on a freighter out of Long Beach for Japan,
and for a couple of years
I was gone.

A PHILOSOPHICAL QUESTION

for Carlos

I'm talking with my neighbor Buzz. He was
a diesel mechanic in the Navy.
We're talking tractors and chainsaws, Cats
(with a capital *C*)
and skid-steer loaders.

It's unlikely
he will ever read the poems
of Jorge Carrera Andrade, or those of Josefina de la Torre,
but it may be
that watching football on TV
is the equivalent of reading poetry.

And who's to say
the one is more ennobling, less self-indulgent
than the other? Who's to say?

TAKING LEAVE OF BEI DAO ON THE SIDEWALK
NEXT TO THE PARKING LOT OF THE OLD CHURCH
IN DOWNTOWN PORTLAND

On Friday you fly back to Sacramento,
where you reside for now. A rare bird, a stray from Asia,
you've flown
all over the world—Beijing
to Oslo, to Ramallah...

Forty years ago,
banished to the countryside,
you worked with concrete on construction sites, and later
became a blacksmith.
(I worked construction, too.)

Tonight, after our public reading—you
reading your poems in Chinese, and I the English versions—
we go to a neighborhood bar
to celebrate,
with Li Jiguang and your old friend Li Tie.

Whether you and I will meet again
is uncertain,
but in parting, you propose we build a house together—
you'll do the concrete work,
I'll do the carpentry.

RIDING THE HIGH BALL

I

I tried contracting for a while
in San Francisco,
but my career as an entrepreneur
was short-lived, and I went back to work out of the hall.
Carpenters Local 483,
the dago local.

Right off, the dispatcher
sends me out to a job site, says for me to see Frank.
Frank says, "Can you work high?"
"Sure," I say, bluffing.
So I got the job, and got to confront, every day
for over a year,
my fear of heights.

2

It was a bridge job.
To get to where the work was, we either climbed
or rode the headache ball,
the high ball.
Like the lead sinker on a fishing line,
this was a solid steel, five-hundred-pound oversize basketball
attached directly above the hook
on the whip line
of a 52-ton truck crane.

Grab the cable, sit on the ball, cross your legs
and pucker up,
squeezing the cable between your thighs. Then signal
the operator, and hang on tight.
Up and away!
Sixty, eighty, a hundred feet in the air, dangling
out over the construction site.

                              3
"There's no rush like the rush you get
from riding the high ball,"
says my partner,
a long-haired druggie, a pile-buck from Oakland,
and he should know.

Fear and glory, that's what it was! Fear
and glory. The kind of job
that won't do much for your resumé, but after work
you can hang up your tool belt
and swagger a little.

SNATCH BLOCKS, CURVE BALLS

When a worn snatch block in the rigging broke loose
it struck me square in the chest
with such force it nearly knocked me overboard.
A few inches higher, it would've done damage
to my physiognomy.

When my wife was diagnosed four years ago
it also caught me by surprise.
But fortunately
it's not like I'm some rookie just up from the minors
who can't handle a major league curve ball.

All will be well is the mantra I keep repeating,
and if not *well*, then at least *over*.
Like the Russian said: "Sure, life is tough, but
fortunately, short."

I'm ambling along, not watching my step,
when all of a sudden I find myself
ignominiously
sprawled out on the asphalt.
Damned if I haven't become a *doddering* old man.
So this is life: skinned knees, a wife
drifting into oblivion,
and a body no longer agile enough to recover
its equilibrium.
But my children are not in jail,
the IRS is not after me,
and the moon is beautiful tonight
tangled in the power lines outside the convenience store
where I've stopped for a can of beer,
to reflect
and to compose this poem.

SOME RANDOM THOUGHTS
ON TURNING 75

Snug in my little rat's nest
of half-digested books and paper, a lifetime's cache
of memorabilia
and junk,
I peer out at the world with a quizzical eye,
still trying to make sense of it.

Of the various schemes for saving the planet,
my choice is: another Ice Age.
What a big chill did for the dinosaurs
could also work
for the Republicans
and other vestiges of reptilian mentality.

Although I was for a time a dues-paying member
of the International
Hod Carriers, Building and Common Laborers Union
of America,
Local No. 435,
I never actually carried a hod.

And although I've been reading the Tibetan
Book of the Dead
aloud at my dying wife's bedside,
as a skeptic I'm not altogether sure this will help her.
But under the circumstances
it can't hurt.

INDIANAPOLIS

In this dream I'm reading a book entitled
Meaninglessness.
On page 369 I discover a passage
which so brilliantly elucidates the meaning of meaninglessness
I resolve to copy it out
in longhand,
to incise it into my brain.

But the thrill at discovering this truth is so intense
I wake up from the dream—
only to realize I've loaned the book to a friend
who was on his way to a conference
in Indianapolis,
and the plane crashed
with the book in his luggage.

I mourn the loss of the book more than the loss of my friend,
and I am so ashamed of this
I wake up again
to realize I've been dreaming again,
and now there is only the sound of the word *Indianapolis*
and a Post-it note stuck on my desk
reading "p. 369."

FIRE AND ICE: AN ODE TO BARBARA STANWYCK

When she was good, she was very, very good,
and when she was bad, she was terrific.

— WALTER MATTHAU

It's the same dame!

— WILLIAM DEMAREST, IN *THE LADY EVE*

You could do worse
than spend your evenings watching Barbara Stanwyck films
on DVD, studying them.
Admittedly, this doesn't have the same cachet among the literati
as reading Proust or Heidegger,
but Art is Art
and Philosophy is where you find it.

In *Golden Boy* she's "a dame from Newark"
who knows a dozen ways
to make a man fall for her.
And once having seen it, who can forget the trip to Indiana
in *Remember the Night*, where she's a shoplifter
out on bail
in the custody of an assistant DA?

Sublime in *The Lady Eve*, a cardsharp on a cruise ship,
she's got poor Henry Fonda wrapped around her little finger.
He doesn't have a clue.
And in that pre-Code gem *Baby Face* she's also
out to get even
as floor by floor in the corporate high-rise
she sleeps her way to the top.

She could play anything:
a gangster's moll or an evangelist,
a madcap heiress or a mail-order bride,
a whip-wielding dominatrix... A centenarian *and* a debutante
in the same movie,
an Old West sharpshooter (in *Annie Oakley*),
a burlesque queen with the moniker "Sugarpuss O'Shea"...

As Phyllis Dietrichson, the femme fatale in *Double Indemnity*,
she's to die for,
and in the end that's what Fred MacMurray does.
Gable, Cooper, Cagney, Bogart, Flynn—she played with them all
and held her own, tough
but vulnerable,
like the orphaned kid from Brooklyn that she was.

At times breathtakingly beautiful,
she could also curl the edges of the screen
with an outburst of invective.
Fire and Ice—
that says it all
for arguably the greatest actress to come out of Hollywood,
the brightest star to shine in the celluloid heavens.

PATRIOT

The man in the motorized wheelchair
waiting to cross the street
is flying an American flag from a long wand
attached to the back of his chair.

Maybe he lost his legs
defending his country, a soldier on foreign soil,
or maybe he'd just been drinking
late one night
and misjudged a curve at high speed.

We don't know, nor do we know
exactly what he's thinking
as he waits in his little conveyance, flag flapping,
for the light to change.

THE BENEFIT OF SMOKING

"Smoking can pay off," says Jerry,
lighting another cigarette and telling how
in 1945, serving aboard a destroyer in the Pacific,
he stepped out on deck once
for a smoke.

Seconds later, a shell
ripped through the bulkhead,
killing his shipmates instantly, and sending him sprawling
across the deck,
shell-shocked but otherwise unharmed.

"So, you see, I wouldn't be here
if I didn't smoke," says Jerry, puffing away, still
bucking the odds at 83.

MISHA

Under the house is where I found him
huddled, barely alive,
a bundle of soft white fur
emitting one last feeble *miaow* as I crawled toward him.
This is how Misha died. My cat. My little pal.

Nine lives, they say. And so I thought
by stroking him and talking to him, murmuring his name
over and over again,
maybe I could love him
back to life.
It didn't work. This must have been his ninth.

While he lay dying on the hearth beside the woodstove
next to me, I finally
dozed off...
and dreamt that he had come alive,
miraculously leaping up and scampering around the room.

My son was with me in the dream,
and together we tried stopping him, afraid
he might harm himself
or disappear.
But then, without speaking, we both realized
he had already left his body.
This was his spirit passing through, on its way out
the open window.

It's good to have a cat. Even better
to have a son.

BOUNDARY DISPUTE

Let's get it right.
That's what I say to the neighbor's lawyer
regarding our long-standing boundary dispute.
Let's rectify the situation.
And so... I'm clearing brush on our property line, preparing
to relocate the fence.

"Measurement began our might," old W.B. proclaimed,
but measuring
in this case involves oak savanna, vine maple, blackberry thickets
and global positioning satellites.
Not to mention a pair of loppers and a chainsaw.

It's not that I object in principle
to irregularity,
but the rigor of geometry has always appealed to me.
It's so unnatural. Such an artifice. Like the construction
words place on things.

So let's get it straight, I reiterate,
and further observe:
                    Better to make peace with your neighbor,
even if he is a real prick,
than to have to fire an occasional salvo
across the DMZ
just to keep the bastard on his toes.

RICKREALL

Marge is in charge of Parts & Service
at Rickreall Farm Supply,
and it's just possible
she knows everything you'd ever want to know
about Kubota tractors.

So, on a sunny afternoon in June,
while the wars in Afghanistan and Iraq drag on
and revolutionary fervor sweeps across North Africa,
I'm on my way to Rickreall
to consult with Marge
about my tractor. The gearshift for the PTO
is jammed.

Immediately she brings up an exploded view
on her computer screen
and pinpoints
the likely cause.
                She looks a little like my mother,
and come to think of it,
my mother's name was Marge.

"Rickreall," by the way, is pronounced "RICK-ree-awl,"
a corruption, some say,
of *Le Créole*, "The Creole," referring
to an early traveler drowned at a ford in the creek—
Rickreall Creek.
But this is disputed.

For a time, because of its large number of Southern
sympathizers,
the place was called "Dixie."

Nowadays, there's not much else to Rickreall
besides Rickreall Farm Supply
with its showroom and lot full of bright orange tractors,
and Marge, of course,
behind the counter.

LONG CREEK, WALLA WALLA

We'd be drinking at a bar in La Grande on a Saturday night,
a few of us from the Duncan section,
when all of a sudden
somebody'd say, "Let's go to Long Creek!"

So we'd pile into the back of his pickup
and drive for hours
through the vast, sagebrush-scented eastern Oregon night
till we came to a cluster of buildings—a tavern
at a crossroads
in the middle of nowhere.

Not a whole lot was happening
in the Long Creek tavern,
which later I learned was called by the locals a "pastime."
Jukebox silent.
Pool table deserted.
One lone cowboy and the barmaid
palavering...

I was trying to figure
why we had come there and what it all meant.
I was new to the West, and distances
were improbable.

. . . . .

Well, who knows what it meant, and who knows
where it was we went
from there.
               Back to work on Monday morning
tamping ballast, lining track,
maintaining the twenty miles of Union Pacific roadbed
known as "the Duncan section."

Other weekends it'd be different.
We'd be drinking at a bar in Pendleton
and suddenly
somebody'd say, "Let's go to Walla Walla!"

DERAILED BY LOVE

At my age you wouldn't think I'd be
derailed by love... But I had no idea
what lay in store for me
at a cabin in the woods off the Matlock-Brady Road.
Not a cabin really,
more like a small castle
ruled over
by a queen with a cloud of snow-white hair.
Fairy tales are not just for children.

How to Be an Adult
in Love is the title of a book I've been reading,
one of those best-seller, self-help, how-to-do-it manuals
that just might change your life.

May Day today. Mayday, mayday!
I'm driving the freeway home from the castle on the creek
and as I pass a couple of RVs hogging the center lane
I try to recall what Rilke
in one of his *Letters to a Young Poet*—which I
first read at 17—
had to say about love.

On second thought, given the circumstances
maybe I'd do better to forget about Rilke
and remember instead
the adage that goes "There's no fool like an old fool!"
or that other one
about an old dog and new tricks.

EL PASO

The high whine of a train whistle
heard at dusk
from the parking lot behind city hall in Corvallis
is all it takes to put me back aboard
a Southern Pacific freight
crossing west Texas on a starry night in early spring
sixty years ago.

Stretched out on the deck of a flatcar
looking up at the sky,
I had the world on a string. I couldn't imagine
the years ahead
that would lead to my being here now,
an old man, telling you this.

When I got off the train in El Paso I knew my life
would never again be the same.

More New Tricks

ANOTHER DAY

Three blue jays (two Steller's and a scrub jay)
not frequently seen together
are perched on the branches of a dead mimosa
jutting out from the overgrown thicket of flowering quince,
a tangle of green dotted with pink.
Three blue jays
on a blustery morning in March...

Almost eighty now, an octogenarian,
I should have some words of wisdom to impart.
But it turns out
the infirmities and indignities of old age—a tin can
tied to a dog's tail, as Yeats says—
are not necessarily
conducive to wisdom.

Now chickadees, nuthatches, finches, and juncos
emerge from the thicket,
and together with me and the jays
they celebrate.
Our various forms of twittering, squawking, and hopping about
attest to our being alive on the planet
at least for another day.

SPLITTING THE BLANKET

Splitting the blanket is like falling in love
in reverse, although Splitting the Blanket could also be
a name for one of the moves
in Tai Chi—like Parting the Wild Horse's Mane
or Grasping the Peacock's Tail.
Arms upraised.
Breathe in. Breathe out.

Sitting here now for the last time
at the Olympic Club in Centralia, where I sat with her
many times before,
and hearing the bartender say as I leave, "See you next time!"
(he not knowing there will be no *next time*),
I'm remembering how
once, standing lookout on the bow of a freighter,
staring into the darkness,
I kept thinking of the girl I had just been with
in Bangkok
and would likely never see again.

"Women are like buses," my son-in-law's grandfather says.
"You miss one, another will come along."
So let's start over.
Breathe in. Breathe out.

LIKE A PILGRIMAGE

Making a little detour
to revisit the town where I had planned
to change my life,
I see the town's the same.
The old hardware store on Tower Street is still there,
and the place we bought that antique cabinet
for the living room...

The drive up Seminary Hill
is steeper than I remember, like the price one pays
(or doesn't pay)
for a love gone south. The house
that was to be a trysting place or, as I liked to think of it,
a love nest,
has seen some changes made by the new owner,
but none that you would find
displeasing.

Quickly now, no need to linger,
I gather my thoughts, stop for gas, then get back
on the freeway,
heading north.

HOW I BECAME A RED SOX FAN

I

Donny Vragel is to blame.
He lived across the street from me. He was ten, I was nine.
He was Catholic, I was Lutheran.
He taught me baseball, the rules of the game:
how to read the box scores, how to keep score, how to figure
batting averages and earned runs.

It was the summer of 1947.
He said I needed to choose a favorite team.
"What are the teams?" I asked. "Well," he explained,
"I'm a Brooklyn Dodgers fan. They're in the National League.
You should pick a team in the other league,
the American League, where last year
the Boston Red Sox won the pennant. You could be
a Red Sox fan."
"Okay," I said. And that was that.

2

Of course I didn't know then
about Johnny Pesky's botched relay
allowing the Cardinals' Enos Slaughter to score all the way from first
on a single
with the winning run
in the seventh game of that '46 World Series.

Nor was I prepared, two years later,
for the cockamamie reasoning of the Red Sox manager who
"on a hunch," he said,
named Denny Galehouse, a bottom-of-the-barrel bullpen pitcher,
to start

against the Indians
in the deciding one-game tie-breaker
at the climax of the '48 season!

(Nearly seventy years later—today, mid-September 2017,
the Red Sox clinging to a three-game lead, with the Yankees
close behind—
I can still feel myself in Miss Moroney's sixth grade
listening to that game.)

3

And the years to follow... the list goes on,
almost too painful to enumerate:
the Bucky Dent pop-fly home run over the Green Monster
at Fenway in '78,
the ground ball through Bill Buckner's crippled legs
in '86 against the Mets...

If you know baseball, you know these stories.
And if you don't, I'm here to tell you
this utter, passionate, benighted, inconsequential silliness
is all because of Donny Vragel.

STARTING FROM LISBON

Writing to me from a sidewalk café in Lisbon,
my friend, an airline pilot,
is waiting, he says, for two refurbished engines to be installed
on the 767 he flies for Aramco
before taking the plane back to Brazil.

*Could this
be the beginning of a poem?* I wonder,
and ask myself, *If it were, where would it go from there?*

Fernando Pessoa, the Portuguese poet
who divided himself into multiple personalities,
assigning to each its own heteronym
and using his own name only for one of them,
never married,
earned his living as a "commercial correspondent,"
drank heavily
and died at 47.

How one thing leads to another, and what *this* has to do
with *that*,
is not always apparent at first.
One day you wake up with a frog in your throat,
next thing you know
the doctor says you've got six months to live,
if you're lucky.

And I haven't even mentioned
Camoëns,
the 500 English archers on the field at Aljubarrota,
the cathedral-toppling earthquake of 1755
and the sinking of the *Lusitania* ...

A SHORT ESSAY ON TROUBLE

"Troubleshooting"
is not exactly the same as "Looking for trouble," although
the two could easily be confused.
                              Once, troubled
by the side effects of a late-life love affair—
sleepless nights, whole days given over to angst, punctuated
by spasms of doubt—
I thought of consulting Maimonides,
the medieval Jewish philosopher who, late in the twelfth century,
compiled the treatise he called *Guide for the Perplexed*.
Written in Arabic, but with Hebrew letters,
it promised to be
a troubleshooting guide if ever there was one.

However, as I was then led to believe,
Maimonides was mainly involved in a lengthy attempt
to confirm Aristotle,
or else, some claimed, secretly
to refute Aristotle.

So I didn't read Maimonides.

Instead, I recalled what my old friend the poet Robert Peterson
had to say about trouble.
"But trouble brought out the best in me," he wrote
in his poem "How I Became a Poet,"
and went on to say:
                              "And poets, I was told, can't be told
how to think, what to feel, or vice versa, & have lots
of trouble. So that's what I became."

While this didn't entirely solve my problem, it certainly
wasn't something I could refute.

CLOTHES MAKE THE MAN

Altered to fit me,
these four pair of nearly new black jeans
formerly belonging to the Alteration Lady's husband,
now deceased,
have served me well for several years.

My father was a natty dresser.
Starched white shirt. Necktie. Pants pressed to a sharp crease.
But even though I take after him in many ways
and emulate him in many others,
I never took to dressing up.

My father-in-law, too, was a dapper man.
In fact, a haberdasher. He sold men's clothes. He also
wrote a book, and a syndicated column
which appeared each week in newspapers around the country,
called *Clothes Make the Man*.

When I consider the sartorial elegance of these two men,
scrupulous in how they dressed to face the world each morning,
I almost feel ashamed
of dressing as casually as I do.

Therefore I offer, in apology, and also in homage,
this poem,
not without its own shabby elegance —
but ordinary, like a pair of sturdy, plain black jeans.

OR MAYBE ISFAHAN

Just back from a trip to Iran,
settling in for the long, dark, damp Oregon winter,
I plan to study Farsi, learn to play the oud,
fall in love with a raven-haired Persian beauty named Afsaneh,
and live out my days
alongside a fountain in a garden
in Kashan.

NOTES

BOOK EPIGRAPH. The *ars poetica* of the Song dynasty critic Wei Tai is taken from A. C. Graham's *Poems of the Late T'ang* (Penguin Classics, 1965).

WILLAMETTE RIVER, MARION STREET BRIDGE... The name of the river and the valley in western Oregon is pronounced to rhyme with *Damn it!* Thus, wil-LAM-mit.

WHAT WE ARE DOING. Miroslav Holub (1923–1998) was the eminent Czech poet also renowned for his work as a scientist in the field of immunology.

READING THE GOSPELS IN THE LEE HOTEL. The rendition of John 9:39 is from E. V. Rieu's translation in *The Four Gospels* (Penguin Classics, 1954).

TWO CHINESE POETS. These sketches are drawn from material contained in Jonathan Chaves's *Mei Yao-ch'en and the Development of Early Sung Poetry* and J. D. Schmidt's *Yang Wan-li*. Chaves's translations of Yang—*Heaven My Blanket, Earth My Pillow*—are also to be recommended.
Li Bai = Li Po (701–762). He was already in Yang's time a legendary figure.

BUTCHERING RABBITS. Cook Ding is a master butcher mentioned in the *Zhuangzi*. So phenomenal is his skill, so attuned is he to the Dao, that despite his having carved up thousands of oxen over a period of nineteen years, he has never had to sharpen his knife.

HONOLULU. During wartime the Military Sea Transportation Service (MSTS), a branch of the US Navy, contracted with commercial steamship companies for transport of war matériel.

CHANGING THE ALTERNATOR BELT ON YOUR 504. That is, on your Peugeot 504. The "Five-oh-four" was the car model manufactured by the French automaker during the 1970s.

IN THE MIDDLE OF THE NIGHT . . . Du Fu = Tu Fu (712–770).

PROTOKOL. "Peach Blossom Spring" is one of the most famous stories in Chinese literature. As originally told by Tao Qian (365–427), a fisherman lost in the mountains comes across a thriving utopian community isolated from the world and embodying the Confucian virtues. After having returned home, the fisherman tries to retrace his path to the Peach Blossom Spring, but cannot find the way.

GANDY DANCING. Burnside Street is skid row in Portland, Oregon.

THE WISDOM OF CAMOUFLAGE. Baal Shem Tov, "Master of the Holy Name," legendary eighteenth-century rabbi, wonder-worker, teacher, and founder of the Hasidic movement among eastern European Jewry. In Hasidism, tales as well as prayers were employed for mystical purposes, and telling a story became a meritorious deed.

BASIC MANEUVERS. Matsuo Bashō (1644–1694) and Kobayashi Issa (1763–1827), two of the greatest Japanese *haiku* poets.
     Takagi Kyozo (1903–1987), a great modern Japanese poet and prose writer who wrote in his Tsugaru dialect as well as in standard Japanese. He pioneered poetry as a *spoken* art.
     Silent Spring is the groundbreaking 1962 exposé by Rachel Carson, warning of the dangers of the use of pesticides such as DDT.

AT SEA. Stopping off a mooring line: "Usually a line is stopped off by the same bitt it is to be belayed upon, but this is not a set rule as a stopper may be used anywhere a line passes through or around a fairlead" (Cornell and Hoffman, *American Merchant Seaman's Manual*, 5th ed., 1964).

TULIPS. Wang Wei (701–761), major Chinese poet of the Tang dynasty, a contemporary of Du Fu and Li Bai.

DECIDING THE COURSE . . . Lu You (1125–1210), major Song dynasty poet, a prolific writer.

THE *PAN-OCEANIC FAITH*. SIU = Seafarers International Union. "Sparks" is the name given to the radio operator aboard a ship. AB = Able-Bodied Seaman, a deck hand.

THE CHINESE WAY. Su Shi (1037–1101) is the great Song dynasty poet, painter, and calligrapher also known by his pen name Su Dongpo.

Fernie is a town in southeastern British Columbia.

ON MY WAY TO WORK . . . Su Dongpo is the pen name of Su Shi. It means "East Slope Su."

ON THE BEACH. The song referred to is "The *Jeannie C.*" by the Canadian folksinger and songwriter Stan Rogers.

OTHERWISE. PBR = Pabst Blue Ribbon beer.

THE AUTHENTICITY OF THE QUR'AN. Jorge Luis Borges (1899–1986) is the great Argentine poet, short-story writer, and critic.

STARTING FROM LISBON. Luis Vaz de Camoëns (1524–1580) is the author of an epic poem, *The Lusíads*, often compared with Virgil's *Aeneid* and regarded as the national epic of Portugal.

The Battle of Aljubarrota in 1385 resulted in a decisive victory for the Portuguese, aided by the English longbowmen, over the forces of Castile and its Aragonese, French, and Italian allies.

ACKNOWLEDGMENTS

Thanks are due the publishers of the books in which these poems first appeared in book form:

Robert and Lysa McDowell at Story Line Press for *Journeyman's Wages* (1995, reprinted 1997 and 2005) and *China Basin* (2002);

Rodger Moody at Silverfish Review Press for *Studying Russian on Company Time* (1999, reprinted 2016);

Paul Hunter at Wood Works for *Traveling Incognito* (letterpress 2003, reprinted digitally 2006) and *Rembrandt, Chainsaw* (letterpress 2011);

Ed Rettig at Oblio Press for *Old Dogs, New Tricks* (letterpress and digitally 2016);

Michael Daley at Empty Bowl for this present volume, *Cathedrals & Parking Lots: Collected Poems*;

and Jerry Reddan at Tangram for numerous letterpress broadsides and for *At Sea* (2008), a letterpress booklet of ten nautical poems.

Of the poets no longer living, whose work I've admired and found worth stealing from, I must first acknowledge my indebtedness to Robert Peterson and Louis Simpson; bows also to Richard Dankleff, fellow poet and mariner, who sailed off the charts; and to that magician and master of the surreal, my first publisher and *patrón*, George Hitchcock.

No acknowledgments would be complete without mention of the many friends who have supported my poetry habit over the years both with their appreciation and critique of the poems and with their love and friendship. They all know who they are.

Four in particular: Ron and Pleuke Boyce, my oldest friends, to whom many of these poems were addressed, early on; Charles Goodrich, my closest friend, whose sharp eyes and ears are always the first to see and hear my poems; and Joseph Bednarik, without whose support and guidance my literary career, such as it is, would hardly exist.

INDEX OF TITLES

Abandoned Waconda Railroad Station, The, 30

Admiring the View, 39

Airlie Road, 144

Ammo Ship, 57

Another Day, 241

Another Poem about Plumbing, 174

At Sea, 141

Authenticity of the Qur'an, The, 210

Basic Maneuvers, 139

Benefit of Smoking, The, 229

Boundary Dispute, 231

Brief Lecture on Door Closers, A, 176

Building Scaffold, 186

Butchering Rabbits, 45

Camber, 202

Cathedral, The, 20

Changing the Alternator Belt on Your 504, 60

China Basin, 115

Chinese Way, The, 178

Chrysanthemums, 53

Clothes Make the Man, 248

Commuting, 59

Cutting the Grass, 47

Deciding the Course My Education Should Take, 149

Derailed by Love, 236

Digging Footings, 156

Dismantling, 66

Driving 99W, Reflecting on War and Solid Waste Disposal, 172

Дружба народов, 94

Eastern Schockrete, 159

Echocardiogram, 199

El Paso, 2397

Falling Off the Roof, I Miss the Falls City Fourth of July Parade and Picnic, 64

Few Words about Hope—and Baseball, A, 195

Fire and Ice: An Ode to Barbara Stanwyck, 226

Foxtrot U-521, 119

Friendship of the Peoples, 90

Gadsky, Elk-Hunting, 188

Gandy Dancing, 119

Girl from Panama, The, 187

Great Books Revisited, The, 208

Grocery Business, 122

Hitchhiking, 196

Honolulu, 56

How I Became a Red Sox Fan, 244

How It Will Be, 63

How to Bury a Dead Horse, 146

Immortality, 202

Indianapolis, 225

In the Meantime, 19

In the Middle of the Night, Waking from a Dream of My Children, I Go Downstairs and Read Du Fu, 65

Introduction to Russian Grammar, An, 205

Invitation, An, 48

It Could Be Worse, 189

I Try to Tune In Charles Goodrich Reading His Poems over the Radio, but Can Only Get the BBC World Service, so I Listen to the News from Albania Instead, 145

Job No. 75-14, 15

Journeyman's Wages, 14

Keats and Shelley, 204

Last Evening, The, 23
Late October, 211
Leaving Los Angeles, 167
Lenin's Typewriter, 82
Lesson in Physics, A, 181
Life, and Nothing More..., 223
Like a Pilgrimage, 243
Linguistics, 148
Little Meditation on Machines, A, 209
Log Trucks and Coyotes, 173
Long Creek, Walla Walla, 234
Looking for a Ship, 216
Looking for Parts, 42
Looking for Work: Seven Poems Instead
    of a Resumé, 155
Maintenance & Repair, 190
Making Do, 78
Man Studying a Map, 24
Mariposa Slim, 158
Me and Maloney, 8
Misha, 230
Moths, 41
Museum of Russian History, The, 86
Neighbors, 185
Nevada City, California, 163
New Orleans, 1958, 162
Niagara Cyclo-Massage, 120
Oil, Paint, and Drug Reporter, 160
On a Clear Day, 25
On a Freighter, Leaving Newport, 191
One of the Locals, 171
On My Way to Work I Pass Bud's Auto
    Wrecking and Think about Su
    Dongpo, 179
On the Beach, 193
On the Eve of Retirement I Have
    This Dream about Going Back to
    Work, 180
On the Hook in Manila, 166
Oregon Three Times, 58
Or Maybe Isfahan, 249
Otherwise, 197

Out of My Head, 27
Panama Canal, The, 54
Pan-Oceanic Faith, The, 164
Patriot, 228
Philosophical Question, A, 218
Plan, The, 155
Poem Written in the Parking Lot of a
    7-Eleven, 62
Politician in a Cowboy Hat, 198
Practising Archery, 49
Protokol, 98
Putting in Footings, 10
Railroad Crossing, 31
Rainer Maria Rilke Goes Construction,
    126
Raising the Grain, 12
Reading the Gospels in the Lee Hotel,
    28
Regarding the Eclipse, 34
Remodeling the House, 11
Report from the Provinces, A, 206
Rickreall, 232
Riding the High Ball, 220
Royal Express, 201
Saga of the *Goodwill,* 192
Sanskrit, 215
Saving Russia, 107
Short Essay on Trouble, A, 247
Slab on Grade, 18
Snatch Blocks, Curve Balls, 222
Snowdrops, 46
Some Random Thoughts on
    Turning 75, 224
Splitting the Blanket, 242
Starting from Lisbon, 246
Studying Russian on Company Time, 74
Sunday Drive, A, 44
Taking Leave of Bei Dao on the
    Sidewalk next to the Parking Lot
    of the Old Church in Downtown
    Portland, 219
Three Sea Stories, 191

Through the Haze, 40
Thucydides, Bill O'Reilly and I Discuss
    Foreign Affairs, 207
Trade, The, 161
Tulips, 143
Tuned In, 26
Two Chinese Poets, 32
Two Photographs, 194
Union Pacific, 157
Unlacing the Boots, 36
What to Say to Your Neurosurgeon, 147

What We Are Doing, 16
Why Buddhists Don't Kill Flies, 142
Why the Old Carpenter Can't Quite
    Make Out What Exactly Is Being
    Said, 175
Why We Are Afraid, 55
Willamette River, Marion St. Bridge:
    Pier 5, General Details, 7
Wisdom of Camouflage, The, 131
Yokohama, 140

INDEX OF FIRST LINES

A broken-down backhoe, 209

Act like you're reading the sports page, 74

Albania is a small country, 145

Altered to fit me, 248

Although heretofore unconsidered, 176

"Another Christmas shot to hell," 141

A precast concrete plant in rural New Jersey, 159

A '60s Volvo ("PARTS CAR"), 179

At dawn the concrete trucks, 18

A telephone solicitor, 131

At my age you wouldn't think I'd be, 236

At 72, still nursing hopes, 215

By actual count there are twenty-eight flies, 142

Call it *sleet* or call it *snow*, 189

Call Mick Wood, 146

Chances are I'll never tell, 34

Donny Vragel is to blame, 244

Drive stakes, shoot grades, 15

Eight hundred years ago, 107

Firs on the hillside, 59

Fore-and-aft rigged, 192

Foreman's name is Ferdinand, 157

Friends, if you'll stop by sometime, 48

From an upstairs window, 173

From Telegraph Hill you can see for miles, 25

George and I work high, 115

Heavy rains. The river swollen, 63

Hummingbirds live in the thicket, 39

I always wanted to go to sea, 216

I have a head, a noble, 27

"I'll go to sea no more," 193

"I'm a carpenter apprentice, 161

I'm ambling along, not watching my step, 223

I'm showing the new guy, 190

I'm sitting in the police station, telling, 98

I'm talking with Mike over coffee, 187

I'm talking with my neighbor Buzz. He was, 218

I'm thinking about Rembrandt, 211

In February my children pick snowdrops, 46

In the checkout line at Safeway, 188

In the one-hundred block of Twelfth Street, 202

In the pump house where I go, 41

In this dream I'm hired, 180

In this dream I'm reading a book entitled, 225

In this group photograph, 194

I tried contracting for a while, 220

I try to imagine Rilke, 126

It was all new to me, 56

I was a cowboy once, 122

I was standing by the side of the road, 196

I was twelve. The war was over, 139

Jake is the superintendent on this job, 10

Job's nearly over, 8

Just back from a trip to Iran, 249

Just turned 20, 31

Keats and Shelley. Shelley and Keats, 204

Leaning on the counter of the local, 42

Let's get it right, 231

Loss of hearing might account for it, 175

Making a little detour, 243

Marge is in charge of Parts & Service, 232

"Maurice" let's call him. And so, 147

Maybe I already know, 149

Mei Yaochen extolled the "even and bland," 32

Mist in the firs. Moss on the oaks, 49

Mostly we hauled asphalt, 57

My family is bored. We have everything, 55

My neighbor, an out-of-work welder, 54

My plan was simple, 155

На столе, 94

New neighbors, 185

Night and the furthest distance; and the sword, 23

No breeze to ruffle the maple leaves, 62

No roof left at all, stone walls, 30

Not for nothing, 160

Now that you've taken to holding the brush, 178

Observing the underside of freeway overpasses, 200

Old stories, poems, the dictionary, 40

Once, flying out of L.A, 167

One by one the old barns are collapsing, 181

On Friday you fly back to Sacramento, 219

On 99W, about halfway, 172

O'Reilly is bad-mouthing the French, 207

Our tour guide speaks in rapid Russian, 86

"Panorama Land" the tourist folders, 28

Poems in Russian and Portuguese, thousands, 148

Retracing the route, 144

Riding at anchor in Manila Bay, 166

"Royal Express," a blue and gold Peterbilt, 201

Six empty vodka bottles on the table, 90

Smack in the public eye, 66

"Smoking can pay off," says Jerry, 229

Snug in my little rat's nest, 224

Sparky's the sawyer, 156

Sparrows and pigeons. No squirrels. Crows. A tank, 82

Spiritual efforts may come to nothing, 19

Splitting the blanket is like falling in love, 242

Still one more month of hope, 195

Stopping off at the Dari Mart in Harrisburg, 197

Summer vacations, traveling with the family, 171

The authenticity of the Qur'an, 210

The closest I ever came, 163

The decree was issued. A cathedral…, 20

The first I ever heard, 158

The first time was on a freight train, 58

The flag at half-mast in front of the courthouse, 206

The heavily jowled, mustachioed man, 198

The highway out of Salem, 44

The high whine of a train whistle, 237

The lot is vacant, 12

The man in the motorized wheelchair, 228

The News is between 94 and 92, 26

The next step was, 11

The night the *Pan-Oceanic Faith* went down, 164

There's a picture I have, 24

The sun slams into us, 7

The way he had it figured, 162

Thirty-seven degrees, 191

"This is how we built scaffold," 186

Three blue jays (two Steller's and a scrub jay), 241

Three yellow tulip petals, 143

To do this the radiator, 60

To kill one with a single blow takes force, 45

Tommy Sotello and I, 120

To the waters of the Willamette I come, 14

Troubles erupt—like a skin rash, 65

"Troubleshooting," 247

Two concrete blocks and a cardboard box, 78

Two days on Burnside was enough, 119

Under the house is where I found him, 230

Unlacing my boots, I ease my feet into moccasins, 36

We'd be drinking at a bar in La Grande on a Saturday night, 234

We were on campus, 208

What we are doing is hard to explain, 16

When a worn snatch block in the rigging broke loose, 222

When I installed this system, 174

When it comes to the rules, 205

When I was in Vancouver, 109

When the power mower quits, 47

With electrodes attached to my chest, 199

Wondering why not a single plum tree grew, 140

Writing to me from a sidewalk café in Lisbon, 246

X-rays negative, I limp across the parking lot, 64

Yang Wanli was much praised, 33

Yellow and orange, so heavy with rain, 53

You could do worse, 226

ABOUT THE AUTHOR

CLEMENS STARCK was born in 1937. A Princeton dropout and former merchant seaman, he has supported his literary and intellectual interests for more than fifty years by working with his hands, mainly as a carpenter and construction foreman. He is the author of six books of poetry and has performed his poems widely throughout the West. A widower, he has three grown children and lives on forty-some acres in the foothills of the Coast Range in western Oregon.

The book is set in Janson Text, a typeface originally created by Hungarian traveling scholar Nicholas Kis in the 1680s while Kis worked in Anton Janson's Amsterdam workshop. Display type is set in Miller, designed by Matthew Carter in 1997. Book design and composition by VJB/Scribe.